Be
Encouraged

BE Books
by Warren Wiersbe

Be Loyal *(Matthew)*
Be Right *(Romans)*
Be Wise *(1 Corinthians)*
Be Encouraged *(2 Corinthians)*
Be Free *(Galatians)*
Be Rich *(Ephesians)*
Be Joyful *(Philippians)*
Be Complete *(Colossians)*
Be Ready *(1 & 2 Thessalonians)*
Be Faithful *(1 & 2 Timothy, Titus)*
Be Confident *(Hebrews)*
Be Mature *(James)*
Be Hopeful *(1 Peter)*
Be Alert *(2 Peter, 2 & 3 John, Jude)*
Be Real *(1 John)*

Be Encouraged

Warren W. Wiersbe

While this book is designed for the reader's personal enjoyment and profit, it is also intended for group study. A Leader's Guide with Victor Multiuse Transparency Masters is available from your local bookstore or from the publisher.

VICTOR

BOOKS a division of SP Publications, Inc.
WHEATON. ILLINOIS 60187

Offices also in
Whitby, Ontario, Canada
Amersham-on-the-Hill, Bucks, England

Second printing, 1985

Unless otherwise noted, Scripture quotations are from the *King James Version*. Other quotations are from the *New American Standard Bible* (NASB), © 1960, 1962, 1968, 1971, 1972, 1973 by the Lockman Foundation, La Habra, California; the *New International Version* (NIV), © 1978 by the New York International Bible Society; *The Living Bible* (TLB), © 1971 by Tyndale House; and *The New Testament in Modern English* (PH), © 1958, 1960, 1972 by J. B. Phillips, Macmillan Publishing Co., Inc. Used by permission.

Recommended Dewey Decimal Classification: 227.3
Suggested Subject Headings: BIBLE. N.T. 2 CORINTHIANS; CHRISTIAN LIFE

Library of Congress Catalog Card Number: 83-51298
ISBN: 0-88207-620-5

VICTOR BOOKS
A division of SP Publications, Inc.
Wheaton, Illinois 60187

CONTENTS

*Dedicated with much appreciation
to
Galen and Jeanette Call,
Robert and Wilma Montgomery,
and
Cedric and Jean Whitcomb*

*...in years past, faithful associates in
ministry;
today,   friends who are an
encouragement and a joy to know*

PREFACE

Discouragement is no respecter of persons. The seasoned saint as well as the beginning believer can suffer periods of discouragement. The mature minister, for that matter, may have more to be discouraged about than the youthful pastor who is just getting started.

The message of 2 Corinthians has been an encouragement to me over the years, and now I want it to be an encouragement to you. Some of this material was taught as a part of my ministry over "Back to the Bible Broadcast," and the response from listeners led me to believe that what Paul wrote centuries ago is still appropriate today.

I want to thank my good friend Jim Adair for his help and encouragement in the production of another "Be" book. It has been a great delight to work with Jim and his Victor Books staff over the years.

If the message of this book encourages you, then be sure to go out and encourage somebody else!

Warren W. Wiersbe

A Suggested Outline of 2 Corinthians

I. PAUL EXPLAINS HIS MINISTRY—1:1—7:16
  A. Triumphant—1:1—2:17
  B. Glorious—3:1-18
  C. Sincere—4:1-18
  D. Believing—5:1-21
  E. Loving—6:1—7:16
II. PAUL ENCOURAGES THEIR GENEROSITY— 8:1—9:15
  (He was receiving an offering for the Jewish saints.)
  A. Principles of "grace giving"—8:1-24
  B. Promises for "grace givers"—9:1-15
III. PAUL ENFORCES HIS AUTHORITY—10:1—13:14
  A. The warrior, attacking the opposition—10:1-18
  B. The spiritual father, protecting the church—11:1-15
  C. The "fool," boasting of suffering—11:16—12:10
  D. The apostle, exercising loving authority—12:11—13:14

1

Down—But Not Out!

2 Corinthians 1:1-11

"You seem to imagine that I have no ups and downs, but just a level and lofty stretch of spiritual attainment with unbroken joy and equanimity. By no means! I am often perfectly wretched and everything appears most murky."

So wrote the man who was called in his day "The Greatest Preacher in the English-speaking World,"—Dr.John Henry Jowett. He pastored leading churches, preached to huge congregations, and wrote books that were best-sellers.

"I am the subject of depressions of spirit so fearful that I hope none of you ever get to such extremes of wretchedness as I go to."

Those words were spoken in a sermon by Charles Haddon Spurgeon whose marvelous ministry in London made him undoubtedly the greatest preacher England ever produced.

Discouragement is no respecter of persons. In fact, discouragement seems to attack the successful far more than the unsuccessful; for the higher we climb, the farther down we can fall. We are not surprised then when we read that the great Apostle Paul was "pressed out of measure" and "despaired even of life" (2 Cor. 1:8). Great as he was in character and ministry, Paul was human just like the rest of us.

Paul could have escaped these burdens except that he had a call from God (1:1) and a concern to help people. He had founded the church at Corinth and had ministered there for a year and a half (Acts 18:1-18). When serious problems arose in the church after his departure, he sent Timothy to deal with them (1 Cor. 4:17) and then wrote the letter that we call First Corinthians.

Unfortunately, matters grew worse and Paul had to make a "painful visit" to Corinth to confront the troublemakers (2 Cor. 2:1ff). Still, no solution. He then wrote "a severe letter" which was delivered by his associate, Titus (2:4-9; 7:8-12). After a great deal of distress, Paul finally met Titus and got the good report that the problem had been solved. It was then that he wrote the letter we call Second Corinthians.

He wrote the letter for several reasons. First, he wanted to encourage the church to forgive and restore the member who had caused all the trouble (2:6-11). He also wanted to explain his change in plans (1:15-22) and enforce his authority as an apostle (4:1-2; chaps. 10—12). Finally, he wanted to encourage the church to share in the special "relief offering" he was taking up for the needy saints in Judea (chaps. 8—9).

One of the key words in this letter is *comfort* or *encouragement.* The Greek word means "called to one's side to help." The verb is used 18 times in this letter, and the noun 11 times. In spite of all the trials he experienced, Paul was able (by the grace of God) to write a letter saturated with encouragement.

What was Paul's secret of victory when he was experiencing pressures and trials? His secret was *God.* When you find yourself discouraged and ready to quit, get your attention off of yourself and focus it on God. Out of his own difficult experience, Paul tells us how we can find encouragement in God. He gives us three simple reminders.

Remember What God Is to You (2 Cor. 1:3)

Paul began his letter with a doxology. He certainly could not sing about his circumstances, but he could sing about the God who is in control of all circumstances. Paul had learned that praise is an important factor in achieving victory over discouragement and depression. "Praise changes things" just as much as "Prayer changes things."

Praise Him because He is God! You find this phrase "blessed be God" in two other places in the New Testament, in Ephesians 1:3 and 1 Peter 1:3. In Ephesians 1:3 Paul praised God for what He did *in the past,* when He "chose us in [Christ]" (v. 4) and blessed us "with all spiritual blessings" (NASB). In 1 Peter 1:3 Peter praised God for *future* blessings and "a living hope" (NASB). But in 2 Corinthians Paul praised God for *present* blessings, for what God was accomplishing then and there.

During the horrors of the Thirty Years' War, Pastor Martin Rinkart faithfully served the people in Eilenburg, Saxony. He conducted as many as 40 funerals a day, a total of over 4,000 during his ministry. Yet out of this devastating experience, he wrote a "table grace" for his children which today we use as a hymn of thanksgiving:

> Now thank we all our God,
> With heart and hands and voices,
> Who wondrous things hath done,
> In whom His world rejoices!

Praise Him because He is the Father of our Lord Jesus Christ! It is because of Jesus Christ that we can call God "Father" and even approach Him as His children. God sees us in His Son and loves us as He loves His Son (John 17:26). We are "beloved of God" (Rom. 1:7) because we are "accepted in the beloved" (Eph. 1:6).

Whatever the Father did for Jesus when He was ministering on earth, He is able to do for us today. We are dear to the Father because His Son is dear to Him and we are citizens of "the kingdom of His dear Son [the Son of His love]" (Col. 1:13). We are precious to the Father, and He will see to it that the pressures of life will not destroy us.

Praise Him because He is the Father of mercies! To the Jewish people, the phrase *father of* means "originator of." Satan is the father of lies (John 8:44) because lies originated with him. According to Genesis 4:21, Jubal was the father of musical instruments, because he originated the pipe and the harp. God is the Father of mercies because all mercy originates with Him and can be secured only from Him.

God in His grace gives us what we do not deserve, and in His mercy He does not give us what we do deserve. "It is of the Lord's mercies that we are not consumed" (Lam. 3:22). God's mercy is *manifold* (Neh. 9:19), *tender* (Ps. 25:6), and *great* (Num. 14:19). The Bible frequently speaks of the *"multitude* of God's mercies" so inexhaustible is the supply (Ps. 5:7; 51:1; 69:13, 16; 106:7, 45; Lam. 3:32).

Praise Him because He is the God of all comfort! The words *comfort* or *consolation* (same root word in the Greek) are repeated 10 times in verses 1-11. We must not think of *comfort* in terms of "sympathy," because sympathy can weaken us instead of strengthen us. God does not pat us on the head and give us a piece of candy or a toy to distract our attention from our troubles. No, He puts strength into our hearts so we can face our trials and triumph over them. Our English word *comfort* comes from two Latin words meaning "with strength." The Greek word means "to come alongside and help." It is the same word used for the Holy Spirit ("the

Comforter") in John 14—16.

God can encourage us by His Word and through His Spirit, but sometimes He uses other believers to give us the encouragement we need (2 Cor. 2:7-8; 7:6-7). How wonderful it would be if all of us had the nickname "Barnabas—son of encouragement"! (Acts 4:36)

When you find yourself discouraged because of difficult circumstances, it is easy to look at yourself and your feelings, or to focus on the problems around you. But the first step we must take is to look by faith to the Lord and realize all that God is to us. "I will lift up mine eyes unto the hills, from whence cometh my help. My help cometh from the Lord, which made heaven and earth" (Ps. 121:1-2).

Remember What God Does for You (2 Cor. 1:4a, 8-11)

To begin with, *He permits the trials to come.* There are ten basic words for suffering in the Greek language, and Paul used five of them in this letter. The most frequently used word is *thlipsis*, which means "narrow, confined, under pressure," and in this letter is translated *affliction* (2:4; 4:17), *tribulation* (1:4), and *trouble* (1:4, 8). Paul felt hemmed in by difficult circumstances, and the only way he could look was up.

In verses 5 and 6, Paul used the word *pathēma*, "suffering," which was also used for the sufferings of our Saviour (1 Peter 1:11; 5:1). There are some sufferings that we endure simply because we are human and subject to pain; but there are other sufferings that come because we are God's people and want to serve Him.

We must never think that trouble is an accident. For the believer, everything is a divine appointment. There are only three possible outlooks a person can take when it comes to the trials of life. If our trials are the products of "fate" or "chance," then our only recourse is to give up. Nobody can control fate or chance. If *we* have to control everything ourselves, then the situation is equally as hopeless. But if *God* is in control, and we trust Him, then we can overcome circumstances with His help.

God encourages us in all our tribulations by teaching us from His Word that it is He who permits trials to come. He encourages us further by reminding us that *He is in control of trials* (1:8). "We were under great pressure, far beyond our ability to endure, so that we despaired even of life" (NIV). Paul was weighed down like a beast of burden with a load too heavy to bear. But God knew just how much Paul could take and He kept the situation in control.

We do not know what the specific "trouble" was, but it was great enough to make Paul think he was going to die. Whether it was peril from his many enemies (see 1 Cor. 15:30-32; Acts 19:21ff), serious illness, or special satanic attack, we do not know; but we do know that God controlled the circumstances and protected His servant. When God puts His children into the furnace, He keeps His hand on the thermostat and His eye on the thermometer (1 Cor. 10:13; 1 Peter 1:6-7). Paul may have despaired of life, but God did not despair of Paul.

God enables us to bear our trials (2 Cor. 1:9). The first thing He must do is show us how weak we are in ourselves. Paul was a gifted and experienced servant of God, who had been through many different kinds of trials (see 4:8-12; 11:23ff). Surely all of this experience would be sufficient for him to face these new difficulties and overcome them.

But God wants us to trust *Him*—not our gifts or abilities, our experience, or our "spiritual reserves." Just about the time we feel self-confident and able to meet the enemy, we fail miserably. "For when I am weak, then am I strong" (12:10).

When you and I die to self, then God's resurrection power can go to work. It was when Abraham and Sarah were as good as dead physically that God's resurrection power enabled them to have the promised son (Rom. 4:16-25). However, "dying to self" does not mean idle complacency, doing nothing and expecting God to do everything. You can be sure that Paul prayed, searched the Scriptures, consulted with his associates, and trusted God to work. The God who raises the dead is sufficient for *any* difficulty of life! He is able, but we must be available.

Paul did not deny the way he felt, nor does God want us to deny our emotions. "We were troubled on every side; without were fightings, within were fears" (2 Cor. 7:5). The phrase "sentence of death" in 1:9 could refer to an official verdict, perhaps an order for Paul's arrest and execution. Keep in mind that the unbelieving Jews hounded Paul's trail and wanted to eliminate him (Acts 20:19). "Perils by my own countrymen" must not be overlooked in the list of dangers (2 Cor. 11:26).

God delivers us from our trials (2 Cor. 1:10). Paul saw God's hand of deliverance whether he looked back, around, or ahead. The word Paul used means "to help out of distress, to save and protect." God does not always deliver us immediately, nor does He deliver each of His children in the same way. James was beheaded, yet Peter was delivered from prison (Acts 12). *Both* were delivered, but in different ways. Sometimes God delivers us *from* our trials, and at other times He delivers us *in* our trials.

God's deliverance was in response to Paul's faith, as well as to the faith of praying people in Corinth (2 Cor. 1:11). "This poor man cried, and the Lord heard him, and saved him out of all his troubles" (Ps. 34:6).

Finally, *God is glorified through our trials* (2 Cor. 1:11). When Paul reported what God had done for him, a great chorus of praise and thanksgiving went up from the saints to the throne of God. The highest service you and I can render on earth is to bring glory to God, and sometimes that service involves suffering. "The gift bestowed" refers to Paul's deliverance from death, a wonderful gift indeed!

Paul was never ashamed to ask Christians to pray for him. In at least seven of his letters, he mentioned his great need for prayer support (Rom. 15:30-32; Eph. 6:18-19; Phil. 1:19; Col. 4:3; 1 Thes. 5:25; 2 Thes. 3:1; Phile. 22). Paul and the believers in Corinth were helping each other (2 Cor. 1:11, 24).

Just recently, a missionary friend told me about the miraculous deliverance of his daughter from what was diagnosed as a fatal disease. At the very time the girl was so ill, several friends in the United States were praying for the family; and God answered prayer and healed the girl. The greatest help we can give to God's servants is "helping together by prayer."

The word *sunupourgeō* translated "helping together" is used only here in the Greek New Testament and is composed of three words: with, under, work. It is a picture of laborers under the burden, working together to get the job accomplished. It is encouraging to know that the Holy Spirit also assists us in our praying and helps to carry the load (Rom. 8:26).

God works out His purposes in the trials of life, if we yield to Him, trust Him, and obey what He tells us to do. Difficulties can increase our faith and strengthen our prayer lives. Difficulties can draw us closer to other Christians as they share the burdens with us. Difficulties can be used to glorify God. So, when you find yourself in the trials of life, remember what God is to you and what God does for you.

Remember What God Does through You (2 Cor. 1:4b-7)
In times of suffering, most of us are prone to think only of ourselves and to forget others. We become cisterns instead of

channels. Yet one reason for trials is so that you and I might learn to be channels of blessing to comfort and encourage others. Because God has encouraged us, we can encourage them.

One of my favorite preachers is Dr. George W. Truett, who pastored the First Baptist Church of Dallas, Texas for nearly 50 years. In one of his sermons, he told about an unbelieving couple whose baby died suddenly. Dr. Truett conducted the funeral and later had the joy of seeing them both trust Jesus Christ.

Many months later, a young mother lost her baby; and again, Dr. Truett was called to bring her comfort. But nothing he shared with her seemed to help her. But at the funeral service, the newly converted mother stepped to the girl's side and said, "I passed through this, and I know what you are passing through. God called me, and through the darkness I came to Him. He has comforted me, and He will comfort you!"

Dr. Truett said, "The first mother did more for the second mother than I could have done, maybe in days and months; for the first young mother had traveled the road of suffering herself."

However, Paul made it clear that we do not need to experience *exactly* the same trials in order to be able to share God's encouragement. If we have experienced God's comfort, then we can "comfort them which are in any trouble" (2 Cor. 1:4b). Of course, if we have experienced similar tribulations, they can help us identify better with others and know better how they feel; but our experiences cannot alter the comfort of God. That remains sufficient and efficient no matter what our own experiences may have been.

Later in 2 Corinthians 12, Paul will give us an example of this principle. He was given a thorn in the flesh—some kind of physical suffering that constantly buffeted him. We do not know what this "thorn in the flesh" was, nor do we need to know. What we do know is that Paul experienced the grace of God and then shared that encouragement with us. No matter what your trial may be, "My grace is sufficient for thee" (12:9) is a promise you can claim. We would not have that promise if Paul had not suffered.

The subject of human suffering is not easy to understand, for there are mysteries to the working of God that we will never grasp until we get to heaven. Sometimes we suffer because of our own sin and rebellion, as did Jonah. Sometimes we suffer to keep us from sinning, as was the case with Paul (2 Cor. 12:7). Suffering can perfect our character (Rom. 5:1-5) and help us to share the character of God (Heb. 12:1-11).

But suffering can also help us to minister to others. In every church, there are mature saints of God who have suffered and experienced God's grace, and they are the great "encouragers" in the congregation. Paul experienced trouble, not as punishment for something he had done, but as preparation for something he was yet *going to do*—minister to others in need. Just think of the trials that King David had to endure in order to give us the great encouragement that we find in the Psalms.

Second Corinthians 1:7 makes it clear that there was always the possibility that the situation might be reversed: the Corinthian believers might go through trials and receive God's grace so that they might encourage others. God sometimes calls a church family to experience special trials in order that He might bestow on them special abundant grace.

God's gracious encouragement helps us *if we learn to endure.* "Patient endurance" is an evidence of faith. If we become bitter or critical of God, if we rebel instead of submit, then our trials will work *against* us instead of *for* us. The ability to endure difficulties patiently, without giving up, is a mark of spiritual maturity (Heb. 12:1-7).

God has to work *in* us before He can work *through* us. It is much easier for us to grow in knowledge than to grow in grace (2 Peter 3:18). Learning God's truth and getting it into our heads is one thing, but living God's truth and getting it into our character is quite something else. God put young Joseph through 13 years of tribulation before He made him second ruler of Egypt, and what a great man Joseph turned out to be! God always prepares us for what He is preparing for us, and a part of that preparation is suffering.

In this light, 2 Corinthians 1:5 is very important: even our Lord Jesus Christ had to suffer! When we suffer in the will of God, we are sharing the sufferings of the Saviour. This does not refer to His "vicarious sufferings" on the cross, for only He could die as a sinless substitute for us (1 Peter 2:21-25). Paul was referring here to "the fellowship of His sufferings" (Phil. 3:10), the trials that we endure because, like Christ, we are faithfully doing the Father's will. This is suffering "for righteousness' sake" (Matt. 5:10-12).

But as the sufferings increase, so does the supply of God's grace. The word *abound* suggests the picture of a river overflowing. "But He giveth more grace" (James 4:6). This is an important principle to grasp: God has ample grace for our every need, *but He will not bestow it in advance.* We come by faith to the throne of grace "that we may obtain mercy, and find grace to help in time of need" (Heb. 4:16). The Greek word means "help when you need it, timely help."

I read about a devoted believer who was arrested for his faith and condemned to be burned at the stake. The night before the execution, he wondered if he would have enough grace to become a human torch; so he tested his courage by putting his finger into the flame of the candle. Of course, it burned him and he pulled his hand back in pain. He was certain that he would never be able to face martyrdom without failing. But the next day, God gave him the grace he needed, and he had a joyful and triumphant witness before his enemies.

Now we can better understand 2 Corinthians 1:9; for, if we could store up God's grace for emergency use, we would be prone to trust ourselves and not "the God of all grace" (1 Peter 5:10). All the resources God gives us may be kept for future use—money, food, knowledge, etc.—but the grace of God cannot be stored away.

Rather, as we experience the grace of God in our daily lives, it is *invested into our lives as godly character.* (See Rom. 5:1-5.) This investment pays dividends when new troubles come our way, for godly character enables us to endure tribulation to the glory of God.

There is a "companionship" to suffering: it can draw us closer to Christ and to His people. But if we start to wallow in self-pity, suffering will create isolation instead of involvement. We will build walls and not bridges.

The important thing is to fix your attention on God and not on yourself. Remember *what God is to you*—"the Father of our Lord Jesus Christ, the Father of mercies, and the God of all comfort" (2 Cor. 1:3). Remember *what God does for you*—that He is able to handle your trials and make them work out for your good and His glory. Finally, remember *what God does through you*—and let Him use you to be an encouragement to others.

2

You Don't Have to Fail!

2 Corinthians 1:12—2:17

In his book, *Profiles in Courage*, John F. Kennedy wrote, "Great crises produce great men and great deeds of courage."

While it is true that a crisis helps to make a person, it is also true that a crisis helps to reveal what a person is made of. Pilate faced a great crisis, but his handling of it did not give him either courage or greatness. How we handle the difficulties of life will depend largely on what kind of character we have; for what life does to us depends on what life finds in us.

In this very personal letter, Paul opened his heart to the Corinthians (and to us) and revealed the trials he had experienced. To begin with, he had been severely criticized by some of the people in Corinth because he had changed his plans and apparently not kept his promise. When Christians misunderstand each other, the wounds can go very deep. Then, there was the problem of opposition to his apostolic authority in the church. One of the members—possibly a leader—had to be disciplined, and this gave Paul great sorrow. Finally, there were the difficult circumstances Paul had to endure in Asia

(2 Cor. 1:8-11), a trial so severe that he despaired of life.

What kept Paul from failing? Other people, facing these same crises, would have collapsed! Yet Paul not only triumphed over the circumstances, but out of them produced a great letter that even today is helping God's people experience victory. What were the spiritual resources that kept Paul going?

A Clear Conscience (2 Cor. 1:12-24)

Our English word *conscience* comes from two Latin words: *com*, meaning "with," and *scire*, meaning "to know." Conscience is that inner faculty that "knows with" our spirit and approves when we do right, but accuses when we do wrong. Conscience is not the Law of God, but it bears witness to that Law. It is the window that lets in the light; and if the window gets dirty because we disobey, then the light becomes dimmer and dimmer. (See Matt. 6:22-23; Rom. 2:14-16.)

Paul used the word *conscience* 23 times in his letters and spoken ministry as given in Acts. "And herein do I exercise myself, to have always a conscience void of offense toward God, and toward men" (Acts 24:16). When a person has a good conscience, he has integrity, not duplicity; and he can be trusted.

Why were the Corinthians accusing Paul of deception and carelessness? Because he had been forced to change his plans. He had originally promised to spend the winter in Corinth "if the Lord permit" (1 Cor. 16:2-8). Paul wanted to gather the offerings that the Corinthians collected for the poor Jewish believers and give the church the privilege of sending him and his associates on their way to Jerusalem.

Much to Paul's regret and embarrassment, he had to change those plans. I sympathize with him, for in my own limited ministry I have sometimes had to change plans and even cancel meetings—and without benefit of apostolic authority! "Plans get you into things," said Will Rogers, "but you have to work your way out." Paul now planned to make *two* visits to Corinth, one on his way into Macedonia, and the other on his way from Macedonia. He would then add the Corinthian collection to that of the Macedonian churches and go on his way to Jerusalem.

Alas, even Plan B had to be scrapped. Why? Because his own loving heart could not endure another "painful visit" (1:23; 2:1-3). Paul had informed the church about his change in plans, but even this did not silence the opposition. They accused him of following "fleshly wisdom" (1:12), of being careless with the will of God (1:17), and of making plans just to please himself. They were saying, "If Paul says or writes one thing, he really means another! His yes is no, and his no is yes."

Misunderstandings among God's people are often very difficult to untangle, because one misunderstanding often leads to another. Once we start to question the integrity of others or distrust their words, the door is opened to all kinds of problems. But, no matter what his accusers might say, Paul stood firm because he had a clear conscience. What he wrote, what he said, and what he lived were all in agreement. And, after all, he had added to his original plan "if the Lord permit" (1 Cor. 16:7, and note James 4:13-17).

When you have a clear conscience, you will live in the light of the return of Jesus Christ (2 Cor. 1:14). "The day of Jesus Christ" refers to that time when Christ appears and takes His church to heaven. Paul was certain that, at the Judgment Seat of Christ, he would rejoice over the Corinthian believers and they would rejoice over him. Whatever misunderstandings there may be today, when we stand before Jesus Christ, all will be forgiven, forgotten, and transformed into glory, to the praise of Jesus Christ.

When you have a clear conscience, you will be serious about the will of God (vv. 15-18). Paul did not make his plans carelessly or haphazardly; he sought the leading of the Lord. Sometimes he was not sure what God wanted him to do (Acts 16:6-10), but he knew how to wait on the Lord. His motives were sincere: he was seeking to please the Lord and not men. When we stop to consider how difficult both transportation and communication were in that day, we can marvel that Paul did not have *more* problems with his busy schedule.

Jesus instructed us to mean what we say. "Say just a simple, 'Yes, I will' or 'No, I won't.' Your word is enough. To strengthen your promise with a vow shows that something is wrong" (Matt. 5:37, TLB). Only a person with bad character uses extra words to strengthen his yes or no. The Corinthians knew that Paul was a man of true character, because he was a man with a clear conscience. During his 18 months of ministry among them, Paul had proved himself faithful; and he had not changed.

When you have a clear conscience, you glorify Jesus Christ (2 Cor. 1:19-20). You cannot glorify Christ and practice deception at the same time. If you do, you will violate your conscience and erode your character; and eventually the truth will come out. The Corinthians were saved because Paul and his friends preached Jesus Christ to them. How could God reveal truth *through false instruments?* The witness and the walk of the minister must go together, for the work that we do flows out of the lives that we live.

There is no yes and no about Jesus Christ. He is God's "eternal yes" to those who trust Him. "For no matter how many promises God has made, they are yes in Christ. And so through Him the Amen is spoken by us to the glory of God" (v. 20, NIV). Jesus Christ reveals the promises, fulfills the promises, and enables us to claim the promises! One of the blessings of a good conscience is that we are not afraid to face God or men, or to claim the promises God gives in His Word. Paul was not guilty of "manipulating" the Word of God in order to support his own sinful practices (see 4:2).

Finally, when you have a clear conscience, you will be on good terms with the Spirit of God (1:21-24). The word *established* is a business term and refers to the guarantee of the fulfilling of a contract. It was the assurance that the seller gave to the buyer that the product was as advertised, or that the service would be rendered as promised.

The Holy Spirit is God's guarantee that He is dependable and will accomplish all that He has promised. Paul was careful not to grieve the Holy Spirit; and, because the Spirit was not convicting him, he knew that his motives were pure and his conscience was clear.

All Christians have been anointed by the Spirit (v. 21). In the Old Testament, the only persons who were anointed by God were prophets, priests, and kings. Their anointing equipped them for service. As we yield to the Spirit, He enables us to serve God and to live godly lives. He gives us the special spiritual discernment that we need to serve God acceptably (1 John 2:20, 27).

The Spirit has also sealed us (2 Cor. 1:22; Eph. 1:13) so that we belong to Christ and are claimed by Him. The witness of the Spirit within guarantees that we are authentic children of God and not counterfeit (Rom. 5:5; 8:9). The Spirit also assures us that He will protect us, because we are His property.

Finally, the Holy Spirit enables us to serve others (2 Cor. 1:23-24), not as "spiritual dictators" who tell others what to do, but as servants who seek to help others grow. The false teachers who invaded the Corinthian church were guilty of being dictators (see 2 Cor. 11), and this had turned the hearts of the people away from Paul, who had sacrificed so much for them.

The Spirit is God's "earnest" (down payment, guarantee, security) that one day we shall be with Him in heaven and possess glorified bodies. (See Eph. 1:14.) He enables us to enjoy the blessings of heaven in our hearts today! Because of the indwelling Holy Spirit, Paul was able to have a clear conscience and face misunderstandings with love and patience. If you live to please people, misunderstandings will depress you; but if you live to please God, you can face misunderstandings with faith and courage.

A Compassionate Heart (2 Cor. 2:1-11)

I have often quoted an anonymous rhyme that perfectly describes one of the most frequent problems we have as the people of God.

> To live above with saints we love,
> Will certainly be glory!
> To live below with saints we know,
> Well, that's another story!

One of the members of the Corinthian church caused Paul a great deal of pain. We are not sure if this is the same man Paul wrote about in 1 Corinthians 5, the man who was living in open fornication, or if it was another person, someone who publicly challenged Paul's apostolic authority. Paul had made a quick visit to Corinth to deal with this problem (2 Cor. 12:14; 13:1) and had also written a painful letter to them about the situation. In all of this, he revealed a compassionate heart. Note the evidences of Paul's love.

First, *he put others first* (2 Cor. 2:1-4). He did not think of his own feelings, but he thought first of the feelings of others. In Christian ministry, those who bring us great joy can also create for us great sorrow; and this was what Paul was experiencing. He wrote them a stern letter, born out of the anguish of his own heart, and bathed in Christian love. His great desire was that the church might obey the Word, discipline the offender, and bring purity and peace to the congregation.

"Faithful are the wounds of a friend, but the kisses of an enemy are deceitful" (Prov. 27:6). Paul knew that his words would wound those he loved, and this brought pain to his heart. But he also knew (as every loving parent knows) that there is a big difference between *hurting* someone and *harming* him. Sometimes those who love us must hurt us in order to keep us from harming ourselves.

Paul could have exercised his apostolic authority and commanded the people to respect him and obey him; but he preferred to minister with patience and love. God knew that Paul's change in plans had as its motive the sparing of the church from further pain (2 Cor. 1:23-24). Love always considers the feelings of others and seeks to put their good ahead of everything else.

But love also *seeks to help others grow* (2 Cor. 2:5-6). It is worth noting that Paul did not mention the name of the man who had opposed him and divided the church family. However, Paul did tell the church to discipline this man *for his own good*. If the person referred to is the fornicator mentioned in 1 Corinthians 5, then these verses indicate that the church did hold a meeting and discipline the man, and that he repented of his sins and was restored.

True discipline is an evidence of love (see Heb. 12). Some young parents with "modern views" of how to raise children refuse to discipline their disobedient offspring because these parents claim they love their children too much. But if they really loved their children, they would chasten them.

Church discipline is not a popular subject or a wide-spread practice. Too many churches sweep such things "under the rug" instead of obeying the Scriptures and confronting the situation boldly by "speaking the truth in love" (Eph. 4:15). "Peace at any price" is not a biblical principle, for there cannot be true spiritual peace without purity (James 3:13-18). Problems that are "swept under the rug" have a way of multiplying and creating even worse problems later on.

The man whom Paul confronted, and whom the church disciplined, was helped by this kind of loving attention. When I was a child, I didn't always appreciate the discipline that my parents gave me, though I must confess that I deserved far more than I received. But now that I look back, I can thank God that they loved me enough to hurt me and hinder me from harming myself. Now I understand what they really meant when they said, "This hurts us more than it hurts you."

Finally, *love forgives and encourages* (2 Cor. 2:7-11). Paul urged the church family to forgive the man, and he gave solid reasons to back up this admonition. To begin with, they were to forgive him for his own sake "lest [he] be swallowed up with overmuch sorrow" (vv. 7-8). Forgiveness is the medicine that helps to heal broken hearts. It was important that the church assure this repentant member of their love.

In my own pastoral ministry, I have shared in meetings where disciplined members have been forgiven and restored to fellowship; and they have been high and holy hours in my life. When a church family assures a forgiven brother or sister that the sin is forgotten and the fellowship restored, there is a sense of the Lord's presence that is wonderful to experience. Every parent who disciplines a child must follow that discipline with assurance of love and forgiveness, or the discipline

You Don't Have to Fail! / 31

will do more harm than good.

They should confirm their love to the forgiven brother *for the Lord's sake* (vv. 9-10). After all, discipline is as much a matter of obedience to the Lord as it is obligation to a brother. The problem was not simply between a sinning brother and a grieving apostle: it was also between a sinning brother and a grieving Saviour. The man had sinned against Paul and the church, but he had most of all sinned against the Lord. When timid church leaders try to "whitewash" situations instead of facing them honestly, they are grieving the heart of the Lord.

Paul gave a third reason: they must forgive the offender *for the church's sake* (v. 11). When there is an unforgiving spirit in a congregation because sin has not been dealt with in a biblical manner, it gives Satan a "beachhead" from which he can operate in the congregation. We grieve the Holy Spirit and "give place to the devil" when we harbor an unforgiving spirit (Eph. 4:27-32).

One of Satan's "devices" is to accuse believers who have sinned so that they feel their case is hopeless. I have had people write me or phone me to ask for help because they have been under satanic oppression and accusation. The Holy Spirit convicts us of sin so that we will confess it and turn to Christ for cleansing; but Satan accuses us of sin so that we will despair and give up.

When an offending brother or sister is disciplined according to the Bible, and repents, then the church family must forgive and restore the member, and the matter must be forgotten and never brought up again. If the church family—or any person in the family—carries an unforgiving spirit, then Satan will use that attitude as a beachhead for new assaults against the church.

Paul was able to overcome the problems that he faced because he had a clear conscience and a compassionate heart.

But there was a third spiritual resource that gave him victory.

A Conquering Faith (2 Cor. 2:12-17)

It appeared in Asia that Paul's plans had completely fallen apart. Where was Titus? What was going on at Corinth? Paul had open doors of ministry at Troas, but he had no peace in his heart to walk through those doors. Humanly speaking, it looked like the end of the battle, with Satan as the victor.

Except for one thing: Paul had a conquering faith! He was able to break out in praise and write, "Thanks be unto God!" (v. 14) This song of praise was born out of the assurances Paul had because he trusted the Lord.

He was sure that God was leading him (2 Cor. 2:14a). The circumstances were not comfortable, and Paul could not explain the detours and disappointments, but he was sure that God was in control. The believer can always be sure that God is working everything together for good, so long as we love Him and seek to obey His will (Rom. 8:28). This promise is not an excuse for carelessness, but it is an encouragement for confidence.

A friend of mine was to meet a Christian leader behind the Iron Curtain and arrange for the publishing of a certain book, but all the arrangements fell through. My friend was alone in a dangerous place wondering what to do next, when he "chanced" to make contact with a stranger—who took him right to the very leaders he wanted to reach! It was the providence of God at work, the fulfilling of Romans 8:28.

Paul was also sure that *God was leading him in triumph* (2 Cor. 2:14b). The picture here is that of the "Roman Triumph," the special tribute that Rome gave to their conquering generals. It was their equivalent of the American "ticker-tape parade."

If a commander-in-chief won a complete victory over the

enemy on foreign soil, and if he killed at least 5,000 enemy soldiers and gained new territory for the Emperor, then that commander-in-chief was entitled to a Roman Triumph. The processional would include the commander riding in a golden chariot, surrounded by his officers. The parade would also include a display of the spoils of battle, as well as the captive enemy soldiers. The Roman priests would also be in the parade, carrying burning incense to pay tribute to the victorious army.

The procession would follow a special route through the city and would end at the Circus Maximus where the helpless captives would entertain the people by fighting wild beasts. It was a very special day in Rome when the citizens were treated to a full-scale "Roman Triumph."

How does this piece of history apply to the burdened believer today? Jesus Christ, our great commander-in-chief, came to foreign soil (this earth) and completely defeated the enemy (Satan). Instead of killing 5,000 persons, He gave life to more than 5,000 persons—to 3,000 plus at Pentecost and to another 2,000 plus shortly after Pentecost (Acts 2:41; 4:4). Jesus Christ claimed the spoils of battle—lost souls who had been in bondage to sin and Satan (Luke 11:14-22; Col. 2:15; Eph. 4:8). What a splendid victory!

The victorious general's sons would walk behind their father's chariot, sharing in his victory; and that is where believers are today—following in Christ's triumph. We do not fight *for* victory; we fight *from* victory. Neither in Asia nor in Corinth did the situation look like victory to Paul, but he believed God—and God turned defeat into victory.

Finally, Paul was sure that *God was using him as He was leading him* (2 Cor. 2:14c-17). As the Roman priests burned the incense in the parade, that odor affected different people in different ways. To the triumphant soldiers, it meant life and victory; but to the conquered enemy, it meant defeat and death. They were on their way to be killed by the beasts.

Using this image of the incense, Paul pictured the Christian ministry. He saw believers as incense, giving forth the fragrance of Jesus Christ in their lives and labors. To God, believers are the very fragrance of Jesus Christ. To other believers, we are the fragrance of life; but to unbelievers, we are the fragrance of death. In other words, the Christian life and ministry are matters of life and death. The way we live and work can mean life or death to a lost world around us.

No wonder Paul cried out, "And who is sufficient for these things?" (v. 16) He gave his answer in the next chapter: "our sufficiency is of God" (3:5). He reminded the Corinthians that his heart was pure and his motives sincere. After all, there was no need to be clever and "peddle" the Word of God, when he was following in the triumphant train of the victorious Saviour! They might misunderstand him, but God knew his heart.

We don't have to fail! Circumstances may discourage us, and people may oppose us and misunderstand us; but we have in Christ the spiritual resources to win the battle: a clear conscience, a compassionate heart, and a conquering faith.

"If God be for us, who can be against us? . . . Nay, in all these things we are more than conquerors through Him that loved us" (Rom. 8:31, 37).

3

From Glory to Glory

2 Corinthians 3

Wherever you find the genuine, you will find somebody promoting the counterfeit. Even art critics have been fooled by fake "masterpieces," and sincere publishers have purchased "valuable manuscripts," only to discover them to be forgeries. Henry Ward Beecher was right when he said, "A lie always needs a truth for a handle to it."

No sooner did the Gospel of God's grace begin to spread among the Gentiles than a counterfeit "gospel" appeared, a mixture of Law and grace. It was carried by a zealous group of people that we have come to call "the Judaizers." Paul wrote his letter to the Galatians to refute their doctrines, and you will find him referring to them several times in 2 Corinthians.

Their major emphasis was that salvation was by faith in Christ *plus* the keeping of the Law (see Acts 15:1ff). They also taught that the believer is perfected in his faith by obeying the Law of Moses. Their "gospel of legalism" was very popular, since human nature enjoys achieving religious goals instead of simply trusting Christ and allowing the Holy Spirit to work. It is much easier to measure "religion" than true righteousness.

Paul looked upon these false teachers as "peddlers" of the Word of God (see 2 Cor. 2:17, NIV), "religious racketeers" who preyed upon ignorant people. He rejected their devious methods of teaching the Bible (4:2), and despised their tendency to boast about their converts (10:12-18). One reason why the Corinthians were behind in their contribution to the special offering was that the Judaizers had "robbed" the church (11:7-12, 20; 12:14).

How did Paul refute the doctrines and practices of these legalistic false teachers? By showing the surpassing glory of the ministry of the Gospel of the grace of God. In 2 Corinthians 3, Paul contrasted the ministry of the Old Covenant (Law) with the ministry of the New Covenant (grace), and he proved the superiority of the New Covenant ministry. Note the contrasts that he presented.

Tables of Stones—Human Hearts (2 Cor. 3:1-3)

The Judaizers boasted that they carried "letters of recommendation" (v. 1, NIV) from the "important people" in the Jerusalem church, and they pointed out that Paul had no such credentials. It is a sad thing when a person measures his worth by what people say about him instead of by what God knows about him. Paul needed no credentials from church leaders: his life and ministry were the only recommendations needed.

When God gave the Law, He wrote it on tables of stone, and those tables were placed in the ark of the covenant. Even if the Israelites could read the two tables, this experience would not change their lives. The Law is an external thing, and people need an *internal* power if their lives are to be transformed. The legalist can admonish us with his "Do this!" or "Don't do that!" but he cannot give us the power to obey. If we do obey, often it is not from the heart—and we end up worse than before!

The ministry of grace changes the heart. The Spirit of God uses the Word of God and writes it on the heart. The Corinthians were wicked sinners when Paul came to them, but his ministry of the Gospel of God's grace completely changed their lives. (See 1 Cor. 6:9-11.) Their experience of God's grace certainly meant more to them than the letters of commendation carried by the false teachers. The Corinthian believers were lovingly written on Paul's heart, and the Spirit of God had written the truth on their hearts, making them "living epistles of Christ."

The test of ministry is changed lives, not press releases or statistics. It is much easier for the legalist to boast, because he can "measure" his ministry by external standards. The believer who patiently ministers by the Spirit of God must leave the results with the Lord. How tragic that the Corinthians followed the boastful Judaizers and broke the heart of the man who had rescued them from judgment.

Death—Life (2 Cor. 3:4-6)

Paul was quick to give the glory to God and not to himself. His confidence ("trust") was in God, and his sufficiency came from God. Paul was a brilliant and well-educated man; yet he did not depend on his own adequacy. He depended on the Lord.

The legalists, of course, told people that any person could obey the Law and become spiritual. A legalistic ministry has a way of inflating the egos of people. When you emphasize the grace of God, you must tell people that they are lost sinners who cannot save themselves. Paul's testimony was, "But by the grace of God I am what I am" (1 Cor. 15:10). No one is sufficient of himself to minister to the hearts of people. That sufficiency can only come from God.

As you read this chapter, note the different names that Paul used for the Old Covenant and the New Covenant as he contrasted them. In verse 6, "the letter" refers to the Old Covenant law, while "the spirit" refers to the New Covenant message of grace. Paul was not contrasting two approaches to the Bible, a "literal interpretation" and a "spiritual interpretation." He was reminding his readers that the Old Covenant law could not give life; it was a ministry of death (see Gal. 3:21). The Gospel gives life to those who believe, because of the work of Jesus Christ on the cross.

Paul was not suggesting that the Law was a mistake or that its ministry was unimportant. Far from it! Paul knew that the lost sinner must be slain by the Law and left helplessly condemned before he can be saved by God's grace. John the Baptist came with a message of judgment, preparing the way for Jesus and His message of saving grace.

A legalistic ministry brings death. Preachers who major on rules and regulations keep their congregations under a dark cloud of guilt, and this kills their joy, power, and effective witness for Christ. Christians who are constantly measuring each other, comparing "results," and competing with each other, soon discover that they are depending on the flesh and not the power of the Spirit. There never was a standard that could transform a person's life, and that includes the Ten Commandments. Only the grace of God, ministered by the Spirit of God, can transform lost sinners into living epistles that glorify Jesus Christ.

Paul's doctrine of the New Covenant was not something that he invented for the occasion. As a profound student of the Scriptures, Paul certainly had read Jeremiah 31:27-34, as well as Ezekiel 11:14-21. In the New Testament, Hebrews 8—10 is the key passage to study. The Old Covenant law, with its emphasis on external obedience, was preparation for the New Covenant message of grace and the emphasis on internal transformation of the heart.

Fading Glory—Increasing Glory (2 Cor. 3:7-11)

This paragraph is the heart of the chapter, and it should be studied in connection with Exodus 34:29-35. Paul did not deny the glory of the Old Covenant law, because in the giving of the Law and the maintaining of the tabernacle and temple services, there certainly was glory. What he affirmed, however, was that the glory of the New Covenant of grace was far superior, and he gave several reasons to support his affirmation.

1. *The New Covenant glory means spiritual life, not death* (2 Cor. 3:7-8). When Moses descended from the mountain, after conversing with God, his face shone with the glory of God. This was a part of the glory of the giving of the Law, and it certainly impressed the people. Paul then argued from the lesser to the greater: if there was glory in the giving of a Law which brought death, how much more glory is there in a ministry that brings life!

Legalists like the Judaizers like to magnify the glory of the Law and minimize its weaknesses. In his letter to the Galatian churches, Paul pointed out the deficiencies of the Law: the Law cannot justify the lost sinner (Gal. 2:16), give a sinner righteousness (2:21), give the Holy Spirit (3:2), give an inheritance (3:18), give life (3:21), or give freedom (4:8-10). The glory of the Law is really the glory of a ministry of death.

2. *The New Covenant glory means righteousness, not condemnation* (2 Cor. 3:9-10). The Law was not given for the purpose of salvation, for there is no salvation through obedience to the Law. The Law produces condemnation, and is the mirror that reveals how dirty our faces really are. But we

cannot wash our faces in the mirror.

The ministry of the New Covenant produces righteousness and changes lives to the glory of God. Man's greatest need is righteousness, and God's greatest gift is righteousness through faith in Jesus Christ. "For if righteousness [comes] by the Law, then Christ is dead in vain" (Gal. 2:21). The person who tries to live under the Law will find himself feeling more and more guilty, and this can produce a feeling of hopelessness and rejection. It is when we trust Christ, and live by faith in God's grace, that we experience acceptance and joy.

Second Corinthians 3:10 states that the Law really "lost its glory" when compared to the surpassing glory of the ministry of God's grace. There simply is no comparison. Sad to say, there are some people who cannot "feel spiritual" unless they carry a weight of guilt. The Law produces guilt and condemnation, for it is like a bond of indebtedness (Col. 2:14), a guardian who disciplines us (Gal. 4:1-5), and a yoke too heavy to bear (Gal. 5:1; Acts 15:10).

3. *The New Covenant glory is permanent, not temporary* (2 Cor. 3:11). The tense of the verb here is very important: "that which is passing away." Paul wrote at a period in history when the ages were overlapping. The New Covenant of grace had come in, but the temple services were still being carried on and the nation of Israel was still living under Law. In A.D. 70, the city of Jerusalem and the temple would be destroyed by the Romans, and that would mark the end of the Jewish religious system.

The Judaizers wanted the Corinthian believers to go back under the Law, to "mix" the two Covenants. "Why go back to that which is temporary and fading away?" Paul asked. "Live in the glory of the New Covenant, which is getting greater and greater." The glory of the Law is but the glory of past history, while the glory of the New Covenant is the glory of present experience. As believers, we can be "changed . . . from glory to glory" (3:18), something that the Law can never accomplish.

The glory of the Law was fading in Paul's day, and today that glory is found only in the records in the Bible. The nation of Israel has no temple or priesthood. If they did build a temple, there would be no Shekinah glory dwelling in the holy of holies. The Law of Moses is a religion with a most glorious past, but it has no glory today. The light is gone; all that remain are shadows (Col. 2:16-17).

Paul has pointed out that the ministry of grace is internal (2 Cor. 3:1-3), it brings life (vv. 4-6), and it involves increasing glory (vv. 7-11). He presented one final contrast to prove the superiority of the New Covenant ministry of grace.

Concealment—Openness (2 Cor. 3:12-18)
The Bible is basically a "picture book," because it uses symbols, similes, metaphors, and other literary devices to get its message across. In this paragraph, Paul used the experience of Moses and his veil to illustrate the glorious freedom and openness of the Christian life under grace. Paul saw in Moses' experience a deeper spiritual meaning than you and I would have seen as we read Exodus 34:29-35.

1. *The historical event* (2 Cor. 3:12-13). When you are a part of a ministry of increasing glory, you can be bold in what you say; and Paul did not hide his boldness. Unlike Moses, Paul had nothing to conceal.

When Moses came down from communing with God, his face shone, reflecting the glory of God. When he spoke to the people, they could see the glory on his face, and they were impressed by it. But Moses knew that the glory would fade away; so, when he finished teaching the people, he put on a veil. This prevented them from seeing the glory disappear; for, after all, who wants to follow a leader who is losing his glory?

The word translated *end* in verse 13 has two meanings: "purpose" and "finish." The veil prevented the people from seeing the "finish" of the glory as it faded away. But the veil also prevented them from understanding the "purpose" behind the fading glory. The Law had just been instituted, and the people were not ready to be told that this glorious system was only temporary. The truth that the covenant of Law was a preparation for something greater was not yet made known to them.

2. *The national application* (2 Cor. 3:14-17). Paul had a special love for Israel and a burden to see his people saved (Rom. 9:1-3). Why were the Jewish people rejecting their Christ? As the missionary to the Gentiles, Paul was seeing many Gentiles trust the Lord, but the Jews—his own people—were rejecting the truth and persecuting Paul and the church.

The reason? There is a "spiritual veil" over their minds and hearts. Their "spiritual eyes" are blinded, so that when they read the Old Testament Scriptures, they do not see the truth about their own Messiah. Even though the Scriptures were read systematically in the synagogues, the Jewish people did not grasp the spiritual message God had given to them. They were blinded by their own religion.

Is there any hope for the lost Children of Israel? Yes, there is! "Nevertheless, when it [the heart] shall turn to the Lord [by trusting Jesus Christ], the veil shall be taken away" (2 Cor. 3:16).

In each of the three churches I have pastored, it has been my joy to baptize Jewish people who have trusted Jesus Christ. It is amazing how their minds open to the Scriptures after they have been born again. One man told me, "It's like scales falling from your eyes. You wonder why everybody doesn't see what you see!" The veil is removed by the Spirit of God and they receive spiritual vision.

But no sinner—Jew or Gentile—can turn to Christ apart from the ministry of the Holy Spirit of God. "Now the Lord is that Spirit" (v. 17). This statement is a bold declaration of the deity of the Holy Spirit: He is God. The Judaizers who had invaded the church at Corinth were depending on the Law to change men's lives, but only the Spirit of God can bring about spiritual transformation. The Law can bring only bondage, but the Spirit introduces us into a life of liberty. "For ye have not received the spirit of bondage again to fear; but ye have received the Spirit of adoption, whereby we cry, 'Abba, Father' " (Rom. 8:15).

As a nation, Israel today is spiritually blind; but this does not mean that individual Jews cannot be saved. The church today needs to recover its lost burden for Israel. We are their debtors, because all the spiritual blessings we have, came through Israel. "Salvation is of the Jews" (John 4:22). The only way we can "pay off" this debt is by sharing the Gospel with them and praying that they might be saved (Rom. 10:1).

3. *The personal application* (2 Cor. 3:18). "But we all, with open face beholding as in a glass the glory of the Lord, are changed into the same image from glory to glory, even as by the Spirit of the Lord." This verse is the climax of the chapter, and it presents a truth so exciting that I marvel so many believers have missed it—or ignored it. You and I can share the image of Jesus Christ and go "from glory to glory" through the ministry of the Spirit of God!

Under the Old Covenant, only Moses ascended the mountain and had fellowship with God; but under the New Covenant, all believers have the privilege of communion with Him. Through Jesus Christ, we may enter into the very holy of holies (Heb. 10:19-20)—and we don't have to climb a mountain!

The "mirror" is a symbol of the Word of God (James 1:22-25). As we look into God's Word and see God's Son, the Spirit transforms us into the very image of God. It is important, however, that we hide nothing from God. We must be open and honest with Him and not "wear a veil."

The word translated *changed* is the same word translated *transfigured* in the accounts of our Lord's transfiguration (Matt. 17; Mark 9). It describes a change on the outside that comes from the inside. Our English word *metamorphosis* is a transliteration of this Greek word. Metamorphosis describes the process that changes an insect from a larva into a pupa and then into a mature insect. The changes come from within.

Moses *reflected* the glory of God, but you and I may *radiate* the glory of God. When we meditate on God's Word and in it see God's Son, then the Spirit transforms us! We become more like the Lord Jesus Christ as we grow "from glory to glory." *This wonderful process cannot be achieved by keeping the Law.* The glory of the Law faded away, but the glory of God's grace continues to increase in our lives.

Keep in mind that Paul was contrasting, not only the Old Covenant with the New, but also the Old Covenant *ministry* with the ministry of grace. The goal of Old Covenant ministry is obedience to an external standard, but this obedience cannot change human character. The goal of New Covenant ministry is likeness to Jesus Christ. Law can bring us to Christ (Gal. 3:24), but only grace can make us like Christ. Legalistic preachers and teachers may get their listeners to conform to some standard, but they can never transform them to be like the Son of God.

The means for Old Covenant ministry is the Law, but the means for New Covenant ministry is the Spirit of God using the Word of God. (By "the Law" I do not mean the Old Testament, but rather the whole legal system given by Moses.

Certainly, the Spirit can use both the Old and New Testaments to reveal Jesus Christ to us.) Since the Holy Spirit wrote the Word, He can teach it to us. Even more, because the Spirit lives in us, He can enable us to obey the Word from our hearts. This is not legal obedience, born of fear, but filial obedience born of love.

Finally, the result of Old Covenant ministry is bondage; but the result of New Covenant ministry is freedom in the Spirit. Legalism keeps a person immature and immature people must live by rules and regulations (see Gal. 4:1-7). God wants His children to obey, not because of an external code (the Law), but because of internal character. Christians do not live under the Law, but this does not mean that we are lawless! The Spirit of God writes the Word of God on our hearts, and we obey our Father because of the new life He has given us within.

The lure of legalism is still with us. False cults prey on professed Christians and church members, as did the Judaizers in Paul's day. We must learn to recognize false cults and reject their teachings. But there are also Gospel-preaching churches that have legalistic tendencies and keep their members immature, guilty, and afraid. They spend a great deal of time dealing with the externals, and they neglect the cultivation of the inner life. They exalt standards and they denounce sin, but they fail to magnify the Lord Jesus Christ. Sad to say, in some New Testament churches we have an Old Testament ministry.

Paul has now explained two aspects of his own ministry: it is triumphant (chaps. 1—2) and it is glorious (chap. 3). The two go together: "Therefore seeing we have this [kind of] ministry, as we have received mercy, we faint not" (4:1).

When your ministry involves the glory of God—you cannot quit!

4

Courage for the Conflict

2 Corinthians 4:1—5:8

The key theme of this section is repeated in verses 1 and 16: "We faint not!" Literally, Paul said, "We do not lose heart!" There were certainly plenty of reasons for discouragement in Paul's situation, yet the great apostle did not quit. What was it that kept him from fainting in the conflicts of life? He *knew what he possessed in Jesus Christ!* Instead of complaining about what he did not have, Paul rejoiced in what he did have; and you and I can do the same thing.

We Have a Glorious Ministry (2 Cor. 4:1-6)

"Therefore, seeing we have *this kind* of ministry" is the literal translation of what Paul wrote. What kind of ministry? The kind described in the previous chapter: a glorious ministry that brings men life, salvation, and righteousness; a ministry that is able to transform men's lives. This ministry is a gift— we receive it from God. It is given to us because of God's mercy, not because of anything we are or we have done. (See 1 Tim. 1:12-17.)

The way you look at your ministry helps to determine how you will fulfill it. If you look upon serving Christ as a burden instead of a privilege, you will be a drudge and do only what is required of you. Some people even look upon service as a punishment from God. When Paul considered the fact that he was a minister of Jesus Christ, he was overwhelmed by the grace and mercy of God. His positive attitude toward the ministry had some practical consequences in his life.

First, *it kept him from being a quitter* (2 Cor. 4:1). He confessed to the Corinthians that his trials in Asia had almost brought him to despair (1:8). In spite of his great gifts and vast experience, Paul was human and subject to human frailties. But, how could he lose heart when he was involved in such a wonderful ministry? Would God have entrusted this ministry to him so that he might fail? Of course not! With the divine calling came the divine enabling; he knew that God would see him through.

A discouraged Methodist preacher wrote to the great Scottish preacher, Alexander Whyte, to ask his counsel. Should he leave the ministry? "Never think of giving up preaching!" Whyte wrote to him. "The angels around the throne envy you your great work!" That was the kind of reply Paul would have written, the kind of reply all of us need to ponder whenever we feel our work is in vain.

Second, *it kept him from being a deceiver* (2 Cor. 4:2-4). "But we have renounced the things hidden because of shame, not walking in craftiness or adulterating the Word of God, but by the manifestation of the truth commending ourselves to every man's conscience in the sight of God" (v. 2, NASB). Paul was certainly alluding to the Judaizers when he wrote these words. Every false teacher today claims to base his doctrine on the Word of God, but false teachers handle God's Word in deceptive ways. You can prove anything by the Bible, provided you twist the Scriptures out of context and reject the witness of your own conscience. The Bible is a book of literature and it must be interpreted according to the fundamental rules of interpretation. If people treated other books the way they treat the Bible, they would never learn anything.

Paul had nothing to hide, either in his personal life or in his preaching of the Word. Everything was open and honest; there was no deception or distortion of the Word. The Judaizers were guilty of twisting the Scriptures to fit their own preconceived interpretations, and ignorant people were willing to follow them.

If Paul was such a faithful teacher of the Word, then why did not more people believe his message? Why were the false teachers so successful in winning converts? Because the mind of the lost sinner is blinded by Satan, and fallen man finds it easier to believe lies than to believe truth. The Gospel "is hid to them that are lost: in whom the god of this world hath blinded the minds of them which believe not, lest the light of the glorious Gospel of Christ, who is the image of God, should shine unto them" (vv. 3-4).

Paul had already explained that the minds of the Jews were "veiled" because of the blindness of their hearts (3:14-16; Rom. 11:25). The minds of the Gentiles are also blinded! Those who are lost ("perishing") cannot understand the message of the Gospel. Satan does not want the glorious light of salvation to shine into their hearts. As the god of this age and the prince of this world (John 12:31), Satan keeps lost sinners in the dark. The sad thing is, Satan uses *religious* teachers (like the Judaizers) to deceive people. Many of the people who today belong to cults were originally members of Christian churches.

The awesome fact that Paul had received this ministry from Christ kept him from being a quitter and a deceiver; but it also kept him from being a promoter (2 Cor. 4:5-6). "We preach not ourselves!" (v. 5) The Judaizers enjoyed preaching about themselves and glorying in their achievements (10:12-18). They were not servants who tried to help people; they were dictators who exploited people.

Paul was certainly a man who practiced genuine humility. He did not trust in himself (1:9) or commend himself (3:1-5) or preach himself (4:5). He sought only to lead people to Jesus Christ and to build them up in the faith. It would have been easy for Paul to build a "fan club" for himself and take advantage of weak people who thrive on associating with great men. The Judaizers operated in that way, but Paul rejected that kind of ministry.

What happens when you share Jesus Christ with lost sinners? The light begins to shine! Paul compared conversion to Creation as described in Genesis 1:3. Like the earth of Genesis 1:2, the lost sinner is formless and empty; but when he trusts Christ, he becomes a new creation (2 Cor. 5:17). God then begins to *form* and *fill* the life of the person who trusts Christ, and he begins to be fruitful for the Lord. God's "Let there be light!" makes everything new.

We Have a Valuable Treasure (2 Cor. 4:7-12)
From the glory of the new creation, Paul moved to the humility of the clay vessel. The believer is simply a "jar of clay"; it is the treasure *within the vessel* that gives the vessel its value. The image of the vessel is a recurring one in Scripture, and from it we can learn many lessons.

To begin with, God has made us the way we are so that we can do the work He wants us to do. God said of Paul, "He is a chosen vessel unto Me, to bear My name before the Gentiles" (Acts 9:15). No Christian should ever complain to God because of his lack of gifts or abilities, or because of his limitations or handicaps. Psalm 139:13-16 indicates that our very genetic structure is in the hands of God. Each of us must accept himself and be himself.

The important thing about a vessel is that it be clean, empty, and available for service. Each of us must seek to become "a vessel unto honor, sanctified [set apart], and meet for the master's use, and prepared unto every good work" (2 Tim. 2:21). We are vessels so that God might use us. We are *earthen* vessels so that we might depend on God's power and not our own.

We must focus on the treasure and not on the vessel. Paul was not afraid of suffering or trial, because he knew that God would guard the vessel so long as Paul was guarding the treasure (see 1 Tim. 1:11; 6:20). God permits trials, God controls trials, and God uses trials for His own glory. *God is glorified through weak vessels.* The missionary who opened inland China to the Gospel, J. Hudson Taylor, used to say, "All God's giants have been weak men who did great things for God because they reckoned on Him being with them."

Sometimes God permits our vessels to be jarred so that some of the treasure will spill out and enrich others. Suffering reveals not only the weakness of man but also the glory of God. Paul presented a series of paradoxes in this paragraph: earthen vessels—power of God; the dying of Jesus—the life of Jesus; death working—life working. The natural mind cannot understand this kind of spiritual truth and therefore cannot understand why Christians triumph over suffering.

Not only must we focus on the treasure and not on the vessel, but we must also focus on the Master and not on the servant. If we suffer, it is for Jesus' sake. If we die to self, it is so that the life of Christ might be revealed in us. If we go through trials, it is so that Christ might be glorified. And all of this is for the sake of others. As we serve Christ, death works in us—but life works in those to whom we minister.

Dr. John Henry Jowett said, "Ministry that costs nothing, accomplishes nothing." He was right. A pastor friend and I once heard a young man preach an eloquent sermon, but it lacked something. "There was something missing," I said to my friend; and he replied, "Yes, and it won't be there until his heart is broken. After he has suffered awhile, he will have a message worth listening to."

The Judaizers did not suffer. Instead of winning lost souls, they stole converts from Paul's churches. Instead of sacrificing for the people, they made the people sacrifice for them (11:20). The false teachers did not have a treasure to share. All they had were some museum pieces from the Old Covenant, faded antiques that could never enrich a person's life.

It has been my experience that many churches are ignorant of the price a pastor pays to be faithful to the Lord in serving His people. This section is one of three sections in 2 Corinthians devoted to a listing of Paul's sufferings. The other two are 6:1-10 and 11:16—12:10. The test of a true ministry is not stars, but scars. "From henceforth let no man trouble me: for I bear in my body the marks [brands] of the Lord Jesus" (Gal. 6:17).

How can we keep from giving up? By remembering that we are privileged to have the treasure of the Gospel in our vessels of clay!

We Have a Confident Faith (2 Cor. 4:13-18)

The phrase *spirit of faith* means "attitude or outlook of faith." Paul was not referring to a special gift of faith (1 Cor. 12:9), but rather to that attitude of faith that ought to belong to every believer. He saw himself identified with the believer who wrote Psalm 116:10, "I believed, and therefore have I spoken." True witness for God is based on faith in God, and this faith comes from God's Word (Rom. 10:17). Nothing closes a believer's mouth like unbelief (see Luke 1:20).

Of what was Paul so confident? That he had nothing to fear from life or death! He had just listed some of the trials that were a part of his life and ministry, and now he was affirming that his faith gave him victory over all of them. Note the assurances that he had because of his faith.

1. *He was sure of ultimate victory* (2 Cor. 4:14). If Jesus Christ has conquered death, the last enemy, then why fear anything else? Men do everything they can to penetrate the meaning of death and prepare for it, yet the world has no answer to death. Until a person is prepared to die, he is not really prepared to live. The joyful message of the early church was the victory of Christ over death, and we need to return to that victorious emphasis. Note too, that Paul also saw a future reunion of God's people when he wrote, "and shall present us with you." Death is the great divider, but in Jesus Christ there is assurance that His people shall be reunited in His presence (1 Thes. 4:13-18).

2. *He was sure that God would be glorified* (2 Cor. 4:15). This verse parallels Romans 8:28 and gives us the assurance that our sufferings are not wasted: God uses them to minister to others and also to bring glory to His name. How is God glorified in our trials? By giving us the "abundant grace" we need to maintain joy and strength when the going gets difficult. Whatever begins with grace, leads to glory (see Ps. 84:11; 1 Peter 5:10).

3. *He was sure that his trials were working for him, not against him* (2 Cor. 4:16-17). "We faint not" (see v. 1) was Paul's confident testimony. What does it matter if the "outward person" is perishing, so long as the "inward person" is experiencing daily spiritual renewal? Paul was not suggesting that the body is not important, or that we should ignore its

warnings and needs. Since our bodies are the temples of God, we must care for them; but we cannot control the natural deterioration of human nature. When we consider all the physical trials that Paul endured, it is no wonder he wrote as he did.

As Christians, we must live a day at a time. No person, no matter how wealthy or gifted, can live two days at a time. God provides for us "day by day" as we pray to Him (Luke 11:3). He gives us the strength that we need according to our daily requirements (Deut. 33:25). We must not make the mistake of trying to "store up grace" for future emergencies, because God gives us the grace that we need when we need it (Heb. 4:16). When we learn to live a day at a time, confident of God's care, it takes a great deal of pressure off of our lives.

Yard by yard, life is hard!

Inch by inch, life's a cinch!

When you live by faith in Christ, you get the right perspective on suffering. Note the contrasts Paul presented in 2 Corinthians 4:17: light affliction—weight of glory; momentary—eternal; working against us—working for us. Paul was writing with eternity's values in view. He was weighing the present trials against the future glory, and he discovered that his trials were actually working *for him.* (See Rom. 8:18.)

We must not misunderstand this principle and think that a Christian can live any way he pleases and expect everything to turn into glory in the end. Paul was writing about trials experienced in the will of God as he was doing the work of God. God can and does turn suffering into glory, but He cannot turn sin into glory. Sin must be judged, because there is no glory in sin.

Second Corinthians 4:16 should be related to 3:18, because both verses have to do with the spiritual renewal of the child of God. Of itself, suffering will not make us holier men and women. Unless we yield to the Lord, turn to His Word, and trust Him to work, our suffering could make us far worse Christians. In my own pastoral ministry, I have seen some of God's people grow critical and bitter, and go from bad to worse instead of "from glory to glory." We need that "spirit of faith" that Paul mentioned in verse 13.

4. *He was sure that the invisible world was real* (2 Cor. 4:18). Dr. A.W. Tozer used to remind us that the invisible world described in the Bible was the only "real world." If we would only see the visible world the way God wants us to see it, we would never be attracted by anything it has to offer (1 John 2:15-17). The great men and women of faith, mentioned in Hebrews 11, achieved what they did because they "saw the invisible" (Heb. 11:10, 13-14, 27).

The things of this world seem so real because we can see them and feel them; but they are all temporal and destined to pass away. Only the eternal things of the spiritual life will last. Again, we must not press this truth into extremes and think that "material" and "spiritual" oppose each other. When we use the material in God's will, He transforms it into the spiritual, and this becomes a part of our treasure in heaven. (More on this in chapters 8—9.) We value the material *because* it can be used to promote the spiritual, and not for what it is in itself.

How can you look at things that are invisible? By faith, when you read the Word of God. We have never seen Christ or heaven, yet we know they are real because the Word of God tells us so. Faith is "the evidence of things not seen" (Heb. 11:1). Because Abraham looked for the heavenly city, he separated himself from Sodom; but Lot chose Sodom because he walked by sight and not by faith (Heb. 11:10; Gen. 13).

Of course, the unsaved world thinks we are odd—perhaps even crazy—because we insist on the reality of the invisible world of spiritual blessing. Yet Christians are content to govern their lives by eternal values, not temporal prices.

We Have a Future Hope (2 Cor. 5:1-8)

"We have this ministry. . . . We have this treasure. . . . We [have] the same spirit of faith. . . . We have a building of God" (4:1, 7, 13; 5:1). What a testimony Paul gave to the reality of the Christian faith!

This "building of God" is not the believer's heavenly home, promised in John 14:1-6. It is his glorified body. Paul was a tentmaker (Acts 18:1-3) and here he used a tent as a picture of our present earthly bodies. A tent is a weak, temporary structure, without much beauty; but the glorified body we shall receive will be eternal, beautiful, and never show signs of weakness or decay. (See Phil. 3:20-21.) Paul saw the human body as an earthen vessel (2 Cor. 4:7) and a temporary tent; but he knew that believers would one day receive a wonderful glorified body, suited to the glorious environment of heaven.

It is interesting to trace Paul's testimony in this paragraph. *We know* (2 Cor. 5:1). How do we know? Because we trust the Word of God. No Christian has to consult a fortune-teller, a Ouiji board, a spiritist, or a deck of cards to find out what the future holds or what lies on the other side of death. God has told us all that we need to know in the pages of His Word. Paul's "we know" connects with his "knowing" in 4:14, and this relates to the resurrection of Jesus Christ. We know that He is alive; therefore, we know that death cannot claim us. "Because I live, ye shall live also" (John 14:19).

If our tent is "taken down" ("dissolved"), we need not fear. The body is only the house we live in. When a believer dies, the body goes to the grave, but the spirit goes to be with Christ (Phil. 1:20-25). When Jesus Christ returns for His own, He will raise the dead bodies in glory, and body and spirit shall be joined together for a glorious eternity in heaven (1 Thes. 4:13-18; 1 Cor. 15:35-58).

We groan (2 Cor. 5:2-5). Paul was not expressing a morbid desire for death. In fact, his statement is just the opposite: he was eager for Jesus Christ to return so that he would be "clothed upon" with the glorified body. He presented three possibilities using the image of the body as a tent: (1) *alive*—residing in the tent; (2) *dead*—unclothed, out of the tent, "naked"; (3) *clothed upon*—the transformation of the body at the return of Christ. Paul was hoping that he would be alive and on the earth at the return of Christ, so that he might not have to go through the experience of death. Paul used a similar picture in 1 Corinthians 15:51–58, and he used the idea of "groaning" in Romans 8:22-26.

The glorified body is called "a building of God, a house not made with hands" in 2 Corinthians 5:1, and "our house which is from heaven" in verse 2. This is in contrast to our mortal bodies which came from the dust of the earth. "And as we have borne the image of the earthy, we shall also bear the image of the heavenly" (1 Cor. 15:49). It is important to note that Paul was not groaning because he was in a human body, but because he longed to see Jesus Christ and receive a glorified body. He was groaning for glory!

This explains why death holds no terrors for the Christian. Paul called his death a "departure" (2 Tim. 4:6). One meaning of this Greek word is "to take down one's tent and move on." But how can we be sure that we shall one day have new bodies like the glorified body of our Saviour? We can be sure because the Spirit lives within us. Paul mentioned the sealing and the earnest of the Spirit in 2 Corinthians 1:22 (see also Eph. 1:13-14). The Holy Spirit dwelling in the believer's body is the "down payment" that guarantees the future inheritance, including a glorified body. In modern Greek, the word translated *earnest* means "engagement ring." The church is engaged to Jesus Christ and is waiting for the Bridegroom to come to take her to the wedding.

We are always confident (2 Cor. 5:6-8). The people of God can be found in one of two places: either in heaven or on earth (Eph. 3:15). None of them is in the grave, in hell, or in any "intermediate place" between earth and heaven. Believers on earth are "at home in the body," while believers who have died are "absent from the body." Believers on earth are "absent from the Lord," while believers in heaven are "present with the Lord."

Because he had this kind of confidence, Paul was not afraid of suffering and trials, or even of dangers. This is not to suggest that he tempted the Lord by taking unnecessary risks, but it does mean that he was willing to "lose his life" for the sake of Christ and the ministry of the Gospel. He walked by faith and not by sight. He looked at the eternal unseen, not the temporal seen (2 Cor. 4:18). Heaven was not simply a *destination* for Paul: it was a *motivation*. Like the heroes of faith in Hebrews 11, he looked for the heavenly city and governed his life by eternal values.

As we review this section of 2 Corinthians, we can see how Paul had courage for the conflict and would not lose heart. He had a glorious ministry that transformed lives. He had a valuable treasure in the earthen vessel of his body, and he wanted to share that treasure with a bankrupt world. He had a confident faith that conquered fear, and he had a future hope that was both a destination and a motivation.

No wonder Paul was "more than conqueror"! (Rom. 8:37)

Every believer in Jesus Christ has these same marvelous possessions and can find through them courage for the conflict.

5

Motives for Ministry

2 Corinthians 5:9-21

What we believe and how we behave must always go together. Paul usually connected *duty* and *doctrine,* because what God has done for us must motivate us to do something for God. Phillips Brooks said, "Christianity knows no truth which is not the child of love and the parent of duty."

"You would have preached a marvelous sermon," a woman said to her pastor, "except for all those 'therefores' at the end!"

Paul would have agreed with the pastor, for he usually used "therefores" and "wherefores" liberally in his letters. In fact, you find them in this section of 2 Corinthians in verses 9, 11, 16, and 17. Paul has moved from explanation to application, and his theme is *motivation for ministry.* His enemies had accused him of using the ministry of the Gospel for his own selfish purposes, when in reality *they* were the ones who were "merchandising" the Gospel (see 4:2; 2:17).

What is the ministry of the Christian? To persuade sinners to be reconciled to God (5:11, 20). We must never force people to trust Christ, or coerce them by some devious approach.

"Our message to you is true, our motives are pure, our conduct is absolutely aboveboard" (1 Thes. 2:3, PH). The Christian worker must have the right motive for ministry as well as the right message.

In this section, Paul stated three acceptable motives for ministry.

The Fear of the Lord (2 Cor. 5:9-13)

"Knowing, therefore, the terror [fear] of the Lord" (v. 11). This kind of attitude is often lacking in ministry. The famous Bible scholar, B.F. Westcott, once wrote, "Every year makes me tremble at the daring with which people speak of spiritual things." Phillips Brooks used to warn about "clerical jesters" whose jesting about the Bible robbed that inspired Book of some of its glory and power. Too often there is a sad absence of reverence in the public meetings of the church, so that it is no surprise that the younger generation is not taking the things of God seriously.

Paul explained this motive by sharing his own testimony in three powerful statements.

We labor (2 Cor. 5:9) means "we are ambitious." There is an ambition that is selfish and worldly, but there is also a holy ambition that honors the Lord. Paul's great ambition was to be well-pleasing to Jesus Christ. The Judaizers ministered to please men and enlisted them in their cause; but Paul ministered to please Jesus Christ alone (Gal. 1:10). A man-pleasing ministry is a carnal, compromising ministry; and God cannot bless it.

The word translated *accepted* ("well-pleasing") is used in several other places in the New Testament, and each of these references helps us better understand what it is that pleases the Lord. It is well-pleasing to Him when we present our bodies to Him as living sacrifices (Rom. 12:1), and when we live so as to help others and avoid causing them to stumble (Rom. 14:18). God is well-pleased when His children separate themselves from the evil around them (Eph. 5:10), as well as when they bring their offerings to Him (Phil. 4:18). He is pleased with children who submit to their parents (Col. 3:20), as well as with saints who permit Jesus Christ to work out His perfect will in their lives (Heb. 13:20-21).

There is nothing wrong with godly ambition. "Yea, so have I strived [been ambitious] to preach the Gospel," was Paul's testimony in Romans 15:20; it was this godly ambition that compelled him to take the message where it had never been heard. Paul commanded the Thessalonian believers to "study [be ambitious] to be quiet" (1 Thes. 4:11). If, led by the Spirit, believers would put as much drive into Christian living and service as they do athletics or business, the Gospel would make a greater impact on the lost world. "I want to be as zealous for God as I was for the devil!" a new Christian told me, and his life was greatly used of God.

We must all appear (2 Cor. 5:10). Not every believer is ambitious for the Lord, but every believer is going to appear before the Lord; and now is the time to prepare. The Judgment Seat of Christ is that future event when God's people will stand before the Saviour as their works are judged and re-warded. (See Rom. 14:8-10.) Paul was ambitious for the Lord because he wanted to meet Him with confidence and not shame (1 John 2:28).

The term *judgment seat* comes from the Greek word *bema*, which was the platform in Greek towns where orations were made or decisions handed down by rulers. (See Matt. 27:19; Acts 12:21; 18:12.) It was also the place where the awards were given out to the winners in the annual Olympic Games. This "judgment seat" must not be confused with the Great White Throne from which Christ will judge the wicked (Rev.

20:11-15). Because of the gracious work of Christ on the cross, believers will not face their sins (Rom. 8:1; John 5:24); but we will have to give an account of our works and service for the Lord.

The Judgment Seat of Christ will be a place of *revelation;* for the word *appear* means "be revealed." As we live and work here on earth, it is relatively easy for us to hide things and pretend; but the true character of our works will be exposed before the searching eyes of the Saviour. He will reveal whether our works have been good or bad ("worthless"). The character of our service will be revealed (1 Cor. 3:13) as well as the motives that impelled us (1 Cor. 4:5).

It will also be a place of *reckoning* as we give an account of our ministries (Rom. 14:10-12). If we have been faithful it will be a place of *reward* and *recognition* (1 Cor. 3:10-15; 4:1-6). For those of us who have been faithful, it will be a time of *rejoicing* as we glorify the Lord by giving our rewards back to Him in worship and in praise.

Is the desire for reward a proper motive for service? The fact that God does promise rewards is proof that the motive is not a sinful one, even though it may not be the highest motive. Just as parents are happy when their children achieve recognition, so our Lord is pleased when His people are *worthy* of recognition and reward. The important thing is not the reward itself, but the joy of pleasing Christ and honoring Him.

We persuade men (2 Cor. 5:11). If God judges His own people, then what will happen to the lost? "And if the righteous scarcely be saved, where shall the ungodly and the sinner appear?" (1 Peter 4:18) The word *terror* does not mean fright, dread, or horror. After all, we are going to see our Saviour—and He loves us. But Paul did not minimize the awesomeness of the occasion. We shall stand before Christ, "and there is no respect of persons" (Col. 3:23-25). Christ has commanded us to spread the Gospel to all nations, and we must be obedient. Someone asked the Duke of Wellington what he thought of foreign missions, and his reply was, "What are your marching orders?"

How can the Christian prepare for the Judgment Seat of Christ? To begin with, he must maintain a clear conscience (2 Cor. 5:11). No doubt some of the enemies at Corinth were saying, "Just wait until Paul stands before the Lord!" But Paul was not afraid, because he knew that his conscience was clear (see 1:12). The truth about each one of us shall be revealed and Jesus Christ will commend us for those things that have pleased Him.

Second, we must take care not to depend on the praise of men (5:12). This verse relates to 3:1, where Paul referred to the "letters of commendation" that the Judaizers prized so highly. If we live only for the praise of men, we will not win the praise of God at the Judgment Seat of Christ. To live for man's praise is to exalt reputation over character, and it is character that will count when we see Christ. Actually, the Corinthians should have commended Paul! Instead, they were "promoting" the Judaizers who gloried in appearance (see 11:18), but were unspiritual in heart.

Finally, we must ignore the criticisms of men (5:13). Paul's enemies said that he was crazy. Paul said that he was "mad" when he was persecuting the church (Acts 26:11), but his enemies said he was "mad" since he had become a believer himself (Acts 26:24). But people said that our Lord was mad, so Paul was in good company (see Mark 3:21). "If I am mad," Paul was saying, "it is for your good and the glory of God—so that makes it worthwhile!"

When Dwight L. Moody was ministering at his large Sunday School and church in Chicago, people often called him "Crazy Moody." In the eyes of the unsaved world, Moody was "crazy" to have given up a successful business career to become a Sunday School worker and evangelist; but time has proved his decision to be a wise one. Today, we don't know the names of the people who laughed at him, but we do know—and honor—the name of D.L. Moody.

It behooves every Christian to examine his own life regularly to see if he is ready for the Judgment Seat of Christ. Wanting to give a good account before Christ is a worthy motive for Christian service.

The Love of Christ (2 Cor. 5:14-17)

How can such opposite emotions as fear and love dwell in the same heart? Certainly they are found in the hearts of children who love their parents and yet respect them and their authority. "Serve the Lord with fear, and rejoice with trembling" (Ps. 2:11).

The phrase "the love of Christ" means His love for us as seen in His sacrificial death. "We love Him, because He first loved us" (1 John 4:19). He loved us when we were unlovely; in fact, He loved us when we were ungodly, sinners, and enemies (see Rom. 5:6-10). When He died on the cross, Christ proved His love for the world (John 3:16), the church (Eph. 5:25), and individual sinners (Gal. 2:20). When you consider the reasons why Christ died, you cannot help but love Him.

He died that we might die (2 Cor. 5:14—"then were all dead"). The tense of the verb gives the meaning "then all died." This truth is explained in detail in Romans 6, the believer's identification with Christ. When Christ died, we died in Him and with Him. Therefore, the old life should have no hold on us today. "I am crucified with Christ" (Gal. 2:20).

He died that we might live (2 Cor. 5:15). This is the positive aspect of our identification with Christ: we not only died with Him, but we also were raised with Him that we might "walk in newness of life" (Rom. 6:4). Because we have died with Christ, we can overcome sin; and because we live with Christ, we can bear fruit for God's glory (Rom. 7:4).

He died that we might live *through* Him: "God sent His only begotten Son into the world, that we might live through Him" (1 John 4:9). This is our experience of salvation, eternal life through faith in Jesus Christ. But He also died that we might live *for* Him, and not live unto ourselves (2 Cor. 5:15). This is our experience of service. It has well been said, "Christ died our death for us that we might live His life for Him." If a lost sinner has been to the Cross and been saved, how can he spend the rest of his life in selfishness?

In 1858, Frances Ridley Havergal visited Germany with her father who was getting treatment for his afflicted eyes. While in a pastor's home, she saw a picture of the crucifixion on the wall, with the words under it: "I did this for thee. What hast thou done for Me?" Quickly she took a piece of paper and wrote a poem based on that motto; but she was not satisfied with it, so she threw the paper into the fireplace. The paper came out unharmed! Later, her father encouraged her to publish it; and we sing it today to a tune composed by Philip P. Bliss.

> I gave My life for thee,
> My precious blood I shed,
> That thou might'st ransomed be,
> And quickened from the dead.
> I gave, I gave, My life for thee,
> What hast thou given for Me?

Christ died that we might live *through* Him and *for* Him, and that we might live *with* Him. "Who died for us, that, whether we wake or sleep, we should live together with Him" (1 Thes. 5:10). Because of Calvary, believers are going to heaven to live with Christ forever!

He died that we might die, and He died that we might live. But He also died that we might *share in the new creation* (2 Cor. 5:16-17). Our new relationship to Christ has brought about a new relationship to the world and the people around us. *We no longer look at life the way we used to.* To know Christ "after the flesh" means to evaluate Him from a human point of view. But "the days of His flesh" are ended (Heb. 5:7) because He has ascended to heaven and is now glorified at the Father's right hand.

Adam was the head of the old creation, and Christ (the last Adam, 1 Cor. 15:45) is the head of the new creation. The old creation was plunged into sin and condemnation because of the disobedience of Adam. The new creation means righteousness and salvation because of the obedience of Jesus Christ. (See Rom. 5:12-21 for the explanation of the "two Adams.") Because we are a part of the new creation, everything has become new.

For one thing, we have a new view of Christ. It is unfortunate that too great an emphasis is given in music and art on Christ "after the flesh." The facts about the earthly life of Jesus are important, because the Christian message is grounded in history. But we must interpret the manger by the throne. We do not worship a Babe in a manger; we worship a glorified Saviour on the throne.

Because "all things are become new," we also have a new view of people around us. We see them as sinners for whom Christ died. We no longer see them as friends or enemies, customers or co-workers; we see them the way Christ sees them, as lost sheep who need a shepherd. When you are constrained by the love of Christ, you want to share His love with others.

During an especially controversial presidential election, a church officer came into a Sunday School class wearing a large pin that promoted one of the candidates. The pastor stopped him and advised him to take it off until he was out of church.

"Why take it off?" he argued. "He's a perfectly good candidate!"

"But suppose the pin is seen by a unsaved man of the other party?" the pastor replied. "Will it upset him and maybe keep him from hearing the Word and getting saved?"

Sullenly, the man removed the pin; and then he smiled and said, "I guess I should remember that people aren't Republicans or Democrats. They're sinners who need a Saviour—and that's more important than winning an election."

But we should also look at other Christians as a part of the new creation, and not evaluate them on the bases of education, race, finances, or position in society. "There is neither Jew nor Greek, there is neither bond nor free, there is neither male nor female: for ye are all one in Christ Jesus" (Gal. 3:28).

The Commission of Christ (2 Cor. 5:18-21)

The key idea in this paragraph is *reconciliation*. Because of his rebellion, man was the enemy of God and out of fellowship with Him. Through the work of the Cross, Jesus Christ has brought man and God together again. God has been reconciled and has turned His face in love toward the lost world. The basic meaning of the word *reconcile* is "to change thoroughly." It refers to a changed relationship between God and the lost world.

God does not have to be reconciled to man, because that was accomplished by Christ on the cross. It is sinful man who must be reconciled to God. "Religion" is man's feeble efforts to be reconciled to God, efforts that are bound to fail. The Person who reconciles us to God is Jesus Christ, and the place where He reconciles us is His cross.

Another key idea in this section is *imputation*. This is a

word borrowed from banking; it simply means "to put to one's account." When you deposit money in the bank, the computer (or the clerk) puts that amount to your account, or to your credit. When Jesus died on the cross, all of our sins were imputed to Him—put to His account. He was treated by God as though He had actually committed those sins.

The result? All of those sins have been paid for and God no longer holds them against us, because we have trusted Christ as our Saviour. But even more: God has put to our account the very righteousness of Christ! "For He hath made Him [Christ] to be sin for us, who knew no sin; that we might be made the righteousness of God in Him" (v. 21).

Reconciliation is based on imputation: because the demands of God's holy Law have been fully met on the cross, God can be reconciled to sinners. Those who believe on Jesus Christ as their Saviour will never have their sins imputed against them again (Rom. 4:1-8; Ps. 32:1-2). As far as their records are concerned, they share the righteousness of Jesus Christ!

There is a lovely illustration of this truth in the little letter Paul wrote to his friend Philemon. Philemon's slave, Onesimus, stole from his master and then fled to Rome. Because of his crimes, he could have been crucified. But in the providence of God, Onesimus met Paul and was converted. Paul wrote the letter to Philemon to encourage his friend to forgive Onesimus and receive him home. "Receive him as myself," wrote Paul (Phile. 17); "if he . . . oweth thee aught, put that on mine account" (v. 18). Paul was willing to pay the bill (imputation) so that Onesimus and Philemon could be reconciled.

How does this wonderful doctrine of reconciliation motivate us to serve Christ? We are ambassadors with a message. God has committed to us the ministry of reconciliation (2 Cor.

5:18) and the word of reconciliation (v. 19).

In the Roman Empire, there were two kinds of provinces: senatorial provinces and imperial provinces. The senatorial provinces were made up of people who were peaceful and not at war with Rome. They had surrendered and submitted. But the imperial provinces were not peaceful; they were dangerous because they would rebel against Rome if they could. It was necessary for Rome to send ambassadors to the imperial provinces to make sure that rebellion did not break out.

Since Christians in this world are the ambassadors of Christ, this means that the world is in rebellion against God. This world is an "imperial province" as far as God is concerned. He has sent His ambassadors into the world to declare peace, not war. "Be ye reconciled to God!" We represent Jesus Christ (2 Cor. 4:5; John 20:21). If sinners reject us and our message, it is Jesus Christ who is actually rejected. What a great privilege it is to be heaven's ambassadors to the rebellious sinners of this world!

When I was a young pastor, it used to embarrass me somewhat to make visits and confront people with the claims of Christ. Then it came to me that I was a privileged person, an ambassador of the King of kings! There was nothing to be embarrassed about. In fact, the people I visited should have been grateful that one of Christ's ambassadors came to see them.

God has not declared war on the world; at the Cross He declared peace. But one day, He *will* declare war; and then it will be too late for those who have rejected the Saviour (2 Thes. 1:3-10). Satan is seeking to tear everything apart in this world, but Christ and His church are involved in the ministry of reconciliation, bringing things back together again, and back to God.

Ministry is not easy. If we are to succeed, we must be

motivated by the fear of the Lord, the love of Christ, and the commission that He has given to us. What a privilege it is to serve Him!

6

Heart to Heart

2 Corinthians 6—7

These two chapters bring to a heartfelt conclusion Paul's explanation of his ministry. He has told his readers that, in spite of trials, his was a triumphant ministry (chaps. 1—2) and a glorious ministry (chap. 3), and that he could not ever think of quitting. His enemies had accused him of using the ministry for personal gain, but he had proved his ministry to be sincere (chap. 4) and based on faith in God (chap. 5). All that remained now was to challenge the hearts of the Corinthians and assure them of his love; and this he did by presenting them with three loving appeals.

An Appeal for Appreciation (2 Cor. 6:1-10)

Principles of Psychology by William James has been a classic text and certainly was a pioneer work in that field. But the author admitted that there was "an immense omission" in the book. "The deepest principle of human nature is the craving to be appreciated," he wrote; and yet he had not dealt with this principle in his book.

As you read 2 Corinthians, you get the strong impression that the church did not really appreciate Paul and the work he had done among them. They should have been defending Paul and not forcing him to defend himself. The Corinthians were boasting about the Judaizers who had invaded the church, and yet the Judaizers had done nothing for them. So Paul reminded them of the ministry God had given him at Corinth.

Paul the evangelist (2 Cor. 6:1-2). It was Paul who had gone to Corinth with the Good News of the Gospel; and through his ministry, the church had been founded. He had fulfilled the work of the "ambassador" described in 2 Corinthians 5:18-21. It was not the Judaizers who had won them to Christ; it was Paul.

But even now, Paul was not certain that everybody in the church who professed to be saved was truly a child of God (see 13:5). He quoted Isaiah 49:8 as his appeal for them to receive God's grace. Because of the reconciling work of Christ on the cross (2 Cor. 5:18-19), today is indeed "the day of salvation." There is no guarantee that any sinner will have the opportunity to be saved *tomorrow.* "Seek ye the Lord while He may be found" (Isa. 55:6).

A pastor was dealing with a young lady who was arguing that she had plenty of time to decide for Jesus Christ. He handed her a piece of paper and said, "Would you sign a statement that you would be willing to postpone salvation for a year?" No, she would not do that. Six months? No again. One month? She hesitated, but said no. Then she began to see the folly of her argument because she had assurance of opportunity *only for today*; and she trusted Christ without delay.

Paul the example (2 Cor. 6:3-20). One of the greatest obstacles to the progress of the Gospel is the bad example of people who profess to be Christians. Unsaved people like to use the inconsistencies of the saints—especially preachers—as an excuse for rejecting Jesus Christ. Paul was careful not to do anything that would put a stumbling block in the way of either sinners or saints (see Rom. 14). He did not want the ministry to be discredited ("blamed") in any way because of his life.

Paul reminded his readers of *the trials he had endured for them* (2 Cor. 6:4-5). He had been a man of endurance ("patience") and had not quit when things were tough. *Afflictions* are trials under pressure, when you are pressed down by circumstances. *Necessities* are the everyday hardships of life, and *distresses* refer to experiences that push us into a corner where there seems to be no escape. The Greek word means "a narrow place."

But even unsaved people go through those experiences, so Paul then listed a few of the trials he endured because of the opposition of people: stripes, imprisonments, and tumults (riots). These he experienced because he was faithfully serving the Lord. He then named some of the sacrifices he made voluntarily for the sake of the ministry: labors (work resulting in weariness), watchings (sleepless nights), fastings (willingly going without food). Of course, Paul had not announced these things publicly. The only reason he mentioned them in this letter was to assure the Corinthians of his love for them.

He further reminded them of the tools he had used in his ministry (6:6-7). *Pureness* means "chastity" (see 11:2). Paul kept himself morally clean. *Long-suffering* refers to patience with difficult people, while *patience* (6:4) refers to endurance in difficult circumstances. Paul depended on the power of the Spirit so that he might manifest the fruit of the Spirit, such as kindness and sincere love. He used the Word of God to convey spiritual knowledge, and he wore the armor of God (see Eph. 6:10ff) to protect him from satanic attacks.

Finally, he reminded them of *the testimony that he bore*

(2 Cor. 6:8-10). Paul listed a series of paradoxes, because he knew that not everybody really understood him and his ministry. Paul's enemies gave an evil report of him as a man who was a dishonorable deceiver. But God gave a good report of Paul as a man who was honorable and true. Paul was well known and yet, at the same time, unknown.

What a price Paul paid to be faithful in his ministry! And yet how little the Corinthians really appreciated all he did for them. They brought sorrow to his heart, yet he was "always rejoicing" in Jesus Christ. He became poor that they might become rich (see 1 Cor. 1:5; 2 Cor. 8:9). The word translated *poor* means "the complete destitution of a beggar."

Was Paul wrong in appealing for their appreciation? I don't think so. Too many churches are prone to take for granted the sacrificial ministry of pastors, missionaries, and faithful church officers. Paul was not begging for praise, but he was reminding his friends in Corinth that his ministry to them had cost him dearly.

Of course, in all of this personal testimony, Paul was refuting the malicious accusations of the Judaizers. How much had *they* suffered for the people at Corinth? What price did *they* pay for their ministry? Like most "cultists" today, these false teachers stole another man's converts; they did not seek to win the lost themselves.

It has well been said, "If you want to find gratitude, look in the dictionary." Are we showing gratitude to those who have ministered to us?

An Appeal for Separation (2 Cor. 6:11—7:1)
In spite of all the problems and heartaches the church had caused him, Paul still loved the believers at Corinth very much. He had spoken honestly and lovingly to them; now he tenderly asked them to open their hearts to him. He felt like a

father whose children were robbing him of the love that he deserved (see 1 Cor. 4:15).

Why were they withholding their love? Because they had divided hearts. The false teachers had stolen their hearts, and now they were cool toward Paul. They were like a daughter engaged to be married, but being seduced by an unworthy suitor (see 2 Cor. 11:1-3). The Corinthians were compromising with the world, so Paul appealed to them to separate themselves to God, the way a faithful wife is separated to her husband.

It is unfortunate that the important doctrine of separation has been misunderstood and abused in recent years, for it is an essential truth. Some sincerely zealous Christians have turned separation into isolation, until their fellowship has become so narrow that they cannot even get along with themselves. In reaction to this extreme position, other believers have torn down all the walls and will fellowship with anybody, regardless of what he believes or how he lives. While we applaud their desire to practice Christian love, we want to remind them that even Christian love must exercise discernment (Phil. 1:9-11).

Paul presented three arguments to try to convince these believers that they must separate themselves from that which is contrary to God's will.

1. The nature of the believer (2 Cor. 6:14-16). It is nature that determines association. Because a pig has a pig's nature, it associates with other pigs in the mud hole. Because a sheep has a sheep's nature, it munches grass with the flock in the pasture. The Christian possesses a divine nature (2 Peter 1:3-4), and therefore he should want to associate himself only with that which pleases the Lord.

The concept of the "unequal yoke" comes from Deuteronomy 22:10, "Thou shalt not plow with an ox and an ass together." The ox was a clean animal to the Jews, but the ass was not (Deut. 14:1-8); and it would be wrong to yoke them together. Furthermore, they have two opposite natures and would not even work well together. It would be cruel to bind them to each other. In the same way, it is wrong for believers to be yoked together with unbelievers.

Note the nouns that Paul used: *fellowship, communion, concord* (harmony), *part, agreement.* Each of these words speaks of having something in common. The word *concord* gives us our English word "symphony," and it speaks of beautiful music that comes when the players are reading the same score and obeying the same leader. What chaos we would have if each instrumentalist played his own tune in his own way!

God's desires for His people are seen in these words. He wants us to *share* with each other (fellowship) and *have in common* (communion) the blessings of the Christian life. He wants us to enjoy *harmony* and *agreement* as we live and work together. When we try to walk with the world and with the Lord at the same time, we break this spiritual fellowship and create discord and division.

Paul saw believers and unbelievers in stark contrast to each other: righteousness—unrighteousness, light—darkness, Christ—Belial (Satan), belief—infidelity (unbelief), God's temple—idols. How could you possibly bring these opposites together? The very nature of the Christian demands that he be separated from that which is unholy. When a saved person marries an unsaved partner, it sets up an impossible situation; and the same thing applies to business partnerships and religious "fellowship."

Note that the word *ye* is plural in 2 Corinthians 6:16. Paul is here referring to the local church as a whole, and not to the individual believer only, as in 1 Corinthians 6:19-20. The local church is the dwelling place of God because believers are the people of God. (See Ezek. 37:26-27; Lev. 26:12; Ex. 6:7; 25:8.) For a local church to compromise its testimony is like a holy temple being defiled.

2. *The command of Scripture* (2 Cor. 6:17). The major part of this quotation is from Isaiah 52:11, but there are also echoes in it of Ezekiel 20:34, 41. The reference in Isaiah is to the captive nation leaving·Babylon and returning to their own land, but the spiritual application is to the separation of the people of God today.

God commands His people to "come out," which implies a definite act on their part. "Be ye separate" suggests devotion to God for a special purpose. Separation is not just a negative act of departure; it is also a positive act of dedication to God. We must separate *from* sin and *unto* God. "Touch not the unclean thing" is a warning against defilement. The Old Testament Jew was defiled if he touched a dead body or the issue from a festering sore. Of course, Christians today do not contract spiritual defilement by touch, but the principle is the same: we must not associate with that which will compromise our testimony or lead us into disobedience.

God's command of separation is found throughout Scripture. He warned Israel not to mingle with the pagan nations in the land of Canaan (Num. 33:50-56); yet they repeatedly disobeyed His Word and were punished because of it. The prophets repeatedly pled with the people to forsake their heathen idols and devote themselves wholly to the Lord. Finally, God had to send Israel into Assyrian captivity and Judah into Babylonian captivity. Our Lord rejected the false "separation" of the Pharisees, but He did warn His disciples against the leaven (false doctrine) of the Pharisees and Sadducees, and He prayed that they would be kept from the defilement of the world (Matt. 16:6, 11; John 17:14-17).

The apostles in their letters to the churches also emphasized doctrinal and personal purity. The believer was *in* the world, but he must be careful not to become like the world. The church must also separate itself from those who reject the doctrine given by Christ and the apostles (Rom. 12:1-2; 16: 17-20; Col. 3:1-2; 1 Tim. 6:10-11; Titus 2:14; 1 Peter 4:3-6; 1 John 4:6). Even in the Book of Revelation, there is an emphasis on God's people being separated from that which is false and contrary to holy living (Rev. 2:14-16, 20-24; 18:4ff).

In our desire for doctrinal and personal purity, we must not become so self-centered that we ignore the needy world around us. Our Lord was "holy, harmless, undefiled, separate from sinners" (Heb. 7:26), and yet He was "a friend of publicans and sinners" (Luke 7:34). Like a skillful physician, we must practice "contact without contamination." Otherwise, we will isolate ourselves from the people who need our ministry the most.

3. The promise of God's blessing (2 Cor. 6:17—7:1). God becomes our Father when we trust Jesus Christ as our Saviour, but He cannot *be to us* a Father unless we obey Him and fellowship with Him. He longs to receive us in love and treat us as His precious sons and daughters. Salvation means we share the Father's life, but separation means that we enter fully into the Father's love. Jesus promised this "deeper love" in John 14:21-23.

God blesses those who separate themselves from sin and unto the Lord. Abraham separated himself from Ur of the Chaldees and God blessed him. When Abraham compromised and went to Egypt, God had to chasten him (Gen. 11:31—12:20). As long as Israel was separated from the sinful nations in Canaan, God blessed them; but when they began to mingle with the heathen, God had to discipline them. Both Ezra and Nehemiah had to teach the people again the meaning of separation (Ezra 9—10; Neh. 9:2; 10:28; 13:1-9, 23-31).

Because of God's gracious promises, we have some spiritual responsibilities (2 Cor. 7:1). We must cleanse ourselves once and for all of anything that defiles us. It is not enough to ask God to cleanse us; we must clean up our own lives and get rid of those things that make it easy for us to sin. No believer can legislate for any other believer; each one knows the problems of his own heart and life.

Too often Christians deal with symptoms and not causes. We keep confessing the same sins because we have not gotten to the root of the trouble and "cleansed ourselves." Perhaps there is "filthiness of the flesh," some pet sin that "feeds" the old nature (Rom. 13:14). Or it may be "filthiness of the spirit," an attitude that is sinful. The prodigal son was guilty of sins of the flesh, but his "moral" elder brother was guilty of sins of the spirit. He could not even get along with his own father. (See Luke 15:11-21.)

But cleansing ourselves is only half of the responsibility; we must also be "perfecting holiness in the fear of God" (2 Cor. 7:1). This is a constant process as we grow in grace and knowledge (2 Peter 3:18). It is important to be balanced. The Pharisees were keen on putting away sin, but they neglected to perfect holiness. But it is foolish to try to perfect holiness if there is known sin in our lives.

Paul had appealed for appreciation and for separation. He gave one final appeal in his attempt to regain the love and devotion of the believers in Corinth.

An Appeal for Reconciliation (2 Cor. 7:2-16)

"Open wide your hearts to us!" (6:13) "Receive us!" (7:2) "Can two walk together, except they be agreed?" (Amos 3:3) If the Corinthians would only cleanse their lives and their church fellowship, God would receive them (2 Cor. 6:17) and they could again have close fellowship with Paul.

The emphasis in this section is on the way God encouraged Paul after he had experienced such great trials in Asia and Troas (see 1:8-10; 2:12-13). There is actually a threefold encouragement recorded in these verses.

1. *Paul encouraged the church* (2 Cor. 7:2-4). The church had received Titus; now they should receive Paul (v. 13). Paul asked them to trust him, for he had never done anything to wrong them. This is certainly a reference to the false teachers who had accused Paul, especially the use of the word *defrauded* ("exploits"—see 11:20, NIV). "Paul is taking up this missionary offering so he can use the money himself!" they were saying.

Why is it so difficult to assure people of our love? What more could Paul do to convince them? He was willing to die for them if necessary, for they were in his heart (see 3:1ff; 6:11-13). He was boasting of them to others ("glorying of you"), but they were criticizing him.

But, in spite of these problems, Paul had good reason to encourage the church because the visit of Titus had been successful; and now there was opportunity to "mend the fences" and restore fellowship. This leads to the second encouragement.

2. *Titus encouraged Paul* (2 Cor. 7:5-10). The first encouragement Paul received was the coming of Titus after they had been separated from each other. It was not easy to communicate or to travel in those days, and Paul had to depend on the providence of God for his plans to work out regarding the visit of Titus to Corinth. (Even with our modern means of transportation and communication, we still need to depend on God's providence.)

But Paul was encouraged by the report that Titus gave of his reception at Corinth. They had read Paul's "painful letter" and had repented of their sins and disciplined the members who had created the problems. It is unfortunate that the *King James Version* translates two different Greek words as "repent," for they have different meanings. The word *repent* in verse 8 means "regret," and *repented* in verse 10 means "to be regretted."

Paul had written them a stern letter, and then had regretted it. But the letter achieved its purpose and the Corinthians repented, and this made Paul rejoice. Their repentance was not merely a passing "regret"; it was a true godly sorrow for sin. "Godly sorrow brings repentance that leads to salvation and leaves no regret, but worldly sorrow brings death" (7:10, NIV). The difference is seen in Judas and Peter. Judas "repented himself" (was full of regret) and went and committed suicide; while Peter wept and repented of his fall (Matt. 26:75—27:5).

Do Christians need to repent? Jesus said that we do (Luke 17:3-4), and Paul agreed with Him (2 Cor. 12:21). Four of the seven churches of Asia Minor, listed in Revelation 2—3, were commanded to repent. To repent simply means "to change one's mind," and disobedient Christians need to repent, not in order to be saved, but in order to restore their close fellowship with God.

3. *The Corinthians encouraged Titus* (2 Cor. 7:11-16). They went to great lengths to do the will of God. First of all, they received Titus and refreshed him by their fellowship (v. 13). They rejoiced his heart as they proved to be all that Paul boasted that they were. They accepted his message from Paul and acted upon it.

In verse 11, Paul spelled out their handling of the matter of discipline. "For behold what earnestness this very thing, this godly sorrow, has produced in you; what vindication of yourselves, what indignation, what fear, what longing, what zeal, what avenging of wrong! In everything you demonstrated yourselves to be innocent in the matter" (NASB). Paul was encouraged when Titus told him of the way they repented and showed concern and zeal to do what was right. Paul assured them that the purpose of his letter was not only to rebuke the offender and help the offended, but to prove his love for the church. Paul had suffered a great deal because of this situation, but his suffering was worth it all now that the problem was solved.

One of the most difficult things to do is to rebuild a shattered relationship. This Paul tried to do in 2 Corinthians, and especially in chapters 6 and 7. Unfortunately, there are many shattered relationships today—in homes, churches, and ministries—and they can be repaired and strengthened only when people face problems honestly, deal with them biblically and lovingly, and seek to get right with God.

As you and I examine our own lives, we must determine to be a part of the answer and not a part of the problem. We must show appreciation, practice separation, and encourage reconciliation if God is to use us to restore broken relationships.

7

The Grace of Giving—Part 1

2 Corinthians 8

One of the major ministries of Paul's third missionary journey was the taking up of a special "relief offering" for the poor Christians in Judea. Once before Paul had assisted in this way (Acts 11:27-30), and he was happy to do it again. It is significant that it was Paul who remembered the "forgotten beatitude" of our Lord: "It is more blessed to give than to receive" (Acts 20:35).

But Paul had other blessings in mind besides the material assisting of the poor. He wanted this offering to strengthen the unity of the church as the Gentile churches shared with the Jewish congregations across the sea. Paul saw the Gentiles as "debtors" to the Jews (Rom. 15:25-28), and the special collection was one way to pay that debt.

This offering was also evidence to the Jewish believers (some of whom were still zealous for the Law) that Paul was not the enemy of the Jews or of Moses (Acts 20:17ff). Early in his ministry, Paul had promised to remember the poor (Gal. 2:6-10), and he labored to keep that promise; but at the same time, he hoped that the generosity of the Gentiles would silence the jealousy of the Jews.

Unfortunately, the Corinthians were not doing their part. Like many people, they had made promises, but they failed to keep them. In fact, an entire year had been wasted (2 Cor. 8:10). What was the cause of this serious delay? The low spiritual level of the church. When a church is not spiritual, it is not generous. Another factor was the invasion of the Judaizers, who probably siphoned off as much money as they could (11:7-12, 20; 12:14).

Paul knew that it would be difficult to get the Corinthians to participate, so he lifted his appeal to the highest spiritual level possible: he taught them that giving was an act of grace. Paul used nine different words to refer to the offering, but the one he used the most was *grace*. Giving is truly a *ministry* and *fellowship* (8:4) that helps others, but the motivation must be from the grace of God in the heart. Paul knew that this collection was a *debt* owed by the Gentiles (Rom. 15:27) and *fruit* from their Christian lives (Rom. 15:28); but it was even more: it was the working of the grace of God in human hearts.

It is a wonderful thing when Christians enter into the grace of giving, when they really believe that giving is more blessed than receiving. How can we tell when we are practicing "grace giving"? Paul indicated that there were a number of evidences that appear when our giving is motivated by grace.

When We Give in Spite of Circumstances (2 Cor. 8:1-2)

The Macedonian churches that Paul was using as an example had experienced severe difficulties, and yet they had given generously. They had not simply gone through "affliction"; they had experienced a "great trial of affliction" (v. 2). They were in *deep poverty,* which means "rock-bottom destitution." The word describes a beggar who has absolutely nothing and has no hope of getting anything. Their difficult situation may have been caused in part by their Christian faith, for they may have lost their jobs or been excluded from the trade guilds because they refused to have anything to do with idolatry.

But their circumstances did not hinder them from giving. In fact, they gave joyfully and liberally! No computer could analyze this amazing formula: great affliction and deep poverty *plus grace* = abundant joy and abounding liberality! It reminds us of the paradox in Paul's ministry: "as poor, yet making many rich" (6:10). It also reminds us of the generous offerings that were taken at the building of the tabernacle (Ex. 35:5-6) and the temple (1 Chron. 29:6-9).

When you have experienced the grace of God in your life, you will not use difficult circumstances as an excuse for not giving. For that matter, are circumstances *ever* an encouragement to giving? In my first pastorate, we had a great need for a new church building; but some of the people opposed a building program because of the "economic situation." Apparently the steel mills were planning to go on strike, and the refineries were going to shut down, and the railroads were having problems . . . and it seemed like a risky time to build. But there were enough people who believed in "grace giving" so that the church did erect a new sanctuary—in spite of the strikes, shutdowns, layoffs, and other economic problems. Grace giving means giving in spite of circumstances.

When We Give Enthusiastically (2 Cor. 8:3-4)
It is possible to give generously but not give enthusiastically. "The preacher says I should give until it hurts," said a miserly church member, "but for me, it hurts just to think about giving!" The Macedonian churches needed no prompting or reminding, as did the church at Corinth. They were more than willing to share in the collection. In fact, *they begged to be*

included! (v. 4) How many times have you heard a Christian *beg* for somebody to take an offering?

Their giving was voluntary and spontaneous. It was of grace, not pressure. They gave because they wanted to give and because they had experienced the grace of God. Grace not only frees us from our sins, but it frees us from ourselves. The grace of God will open your heart *and your hand.* Your giving is not the result of cold calculation, but of warmhearted jubilation!

When We Give as Jesus Gave (2 Cor. 8:5-9)

Jesus Christ is always the preeminent example for the believer to follow, whether in service, suffering, or sacrifice. Like Jesus Christ, the Macedonian Christians *gave themselves to God and to others* (v. 5). If we give ourselves to God, we will have little problem giving our substance to God. If we give ourselves to God, we will also give of ourselves for others. It is impossible to love God and ignore the needs of your neighbor. Jesus Christ gave Himself for us (Gal. 1:4; 2:20). Should we not give ourselves to Him? He died so that we might not live for ourselves, but for Him and for others (2 Cor. 5:15).

The Macedonians' giving was, like Christ's, *motivated by love* (8:7-8). What a rebuke to the Corinthians who were so enriched with spiritual blessings (1 Cor. 1:4-5). They were so wrapped up in the *gifts* of the Spirit that they had neglected the *graces* of the Spirit, including the grace of giving. The Macedonian churches had an "abundance of deep poverty" (2 Cor. 8:2), and yet they abounded in their liberality. The Corinthians had an abundance of spiritual gifts, yet they were lax in keeping their promise and sharing in the collection.

We must never argue that the ministry of our spiritual gifts is a substitute for generous giving. "I teach a Sunday School class, so I don't have to give!" is not an explanation—it's an excuse. The Christian who remembers that his gifts are *gifts* will be motivated to give to others and not "hide" behind his ministry for the Lord. I have met pastors and missionaries who have argued that, since they devote their whole time in serving the Lord, they are not obligated to give. Paul argued just the opposite: since you are wonderfully gifted from God, you ought to want to give even more!

Paul was careful that they understood that he was not *ordering* them to give. Actually, he was contrasting the attitude of the Macedonians with that of the Corinthians. He was pointing out that the Macedonians were following the example of the Lord: they were poor, yet they gave. The Corinthians said that they loved Paul; now he asked them to prove that love by sharing in the offering. Grace giving is an evidence of love—love for Christ, love for God's servants who have ministered to us, and love for those who have special needs that we are able to help meet.

Finally, *their giving was sacrificial* (v. 9). In what ways was Jesus rich? Certainly He was rich in His Person, for He is eternal God. He is rich in His possessions and in His position as King of kings and Lord of lords. He is rich in His power, for He can do anything. Yet, in spite of the fact that He had all these riches—and more—*He became poor.*

The tense of the verb indicates that it is His incarnation, His birth at Bethlehem, that is meant here. He united Himself to mankind and took upon Himself a human body. He left the throne to become a servant. He laid aside all His possessions so that He did not even have a place to lay His head. His ultimate experience of poverty was when He was made sin for us on the cross. Hell is eternal poverty, and on the cross Jesus Christ became the poorest of the poor.

Why did He do it? That we might become rich! This suggests that we were poor before we met Jesus Christ, and we were—totally bankrupt. But now that we have trusted Him, we share in all of His riches! We are now the children of God, "heirs of God, and joint-heirs with Jesus Christ" (Rom. 8:17). Since this is true, *how can we refuse to give to others?* He became poor to make us rich! Can we not follow His example, as did the Macedonian churches, who out of their deep poverty abounded in liberality?

When We Give Willingly (2 Cor. 8:10-12)
There is a great difference between *promise* and *performance*. The Corinthians had boasted to Titus a year before that they would share in the special collection (v. 6), but they did not keep their promise. Note that in verses 10-12 Paul emphasizes *willingness*. Grace giving must come from a willing heart; it cannot be coerced or forced.

During my years of ministry, I have endured many offering appeals. I have listened to pathetic tales about unbelievable needs. I have forced myself to laugh at old jokes that were supposed to make it easier for me to part with my money. I have been scolded, shamed, and almost threatened, and I must confess that none of these approaches has ever stirred me to give more than I planned to give. In fact, more than once I gave *less* because I was so disgusted with the worldly approach. (However, I have never gotten like Mark Twain, who said that he was so sickened by the long appeal that he not only did not give what he planned to give, but he took a bill out of the plate!)

We must be careful here not to confuse *willing* with *doing*, because the two must go together. If the willing is sincere and in the will of God, then there must be "a performance also" (v. 11; Phil. 2:12-13). Paul did not say that *willing* was a substitute for *doing*, because it is not. But if our giving is motivated by grace, we will give willingly, and not because we have been forced to give.

God sees the "heart gift" and not the "hand gift." If the heart wanted to give more, but was unable to do so, God sees it and records it accordingly. But if the hand gives more than the heart wants to give, God records what is in the heart, no matter how big the offering in the hand might be.

A friend of mine was leaving for a business trip, and his wife reminded him before church that she needed some extra money for household expenses. Just before the offering, he slipped some money into her hand; and she, thinking it was their weekly offering, put it all in the plate. It was the expense money for the week.

"Well," said my friend, "we gave it to the Lord and He keeps the records."

"How much did you *intend* to give?" asked their pastor, and my friend gave an amount. "Then that's what God recorded," said the pastor, "because He saw the intent of your heart!"

God sees, not the portion, but the proportion. If we could have given more, and did not, God notes it. If we wanted to give more, and could not, God also notes that. When we give willingly, according to what we have, we are practicing grace giving.

When We Give by Faith (2 Cor. 8:13-24)

Paul did not suggest that the rich become poor so that the poor might become rich. It would be unwise for a Christian to go into debt in order to relieve somebody else's debt, unless, of course, he was able to handle the responsibility of paying the debt back. Paul saw an "equality" in the whole procedure: the Gentiles were enriched spiritually by the Jews, so the Jews should be enriched materially by the Gentiles (see Rom. 15:25-28). Furthermore, the Gentile churches at that time were enjoying some measure of material wealth, while the believers in Judea were suffering. That situation could one day be reversed. There might come a time when the Jewish believers would be assisting the Gentiles.

Who does the equalizing? God does. Paul used the miracle of the manna as an illustration of the principle (Ex. 16:18). No matter how much manna the Jews gathered each day, they always had what they needed. Those who tried to hoard the manna discovered that it was impossible, because the manna would decay and smell (Ex. 16:20). The lesson is clear: gather what you need, share what you can, and don't try to hoard God's blessings. God will see to it that you will not be in need if you trust Him and obey His Word.

Our *motive* for giving is God's spiritual blessing in our lives, but our *measure* for giving is God's material blessing. Paul made this clear when he wrote to the Corinthians in his first letter, "Let every one of you lay by him in store, as God hath prospered him" (1 Cor. 16:2). Paul did not lay down any mathematical formula, because grace giving is not limited by a tithe (10 percent). Grace giving is systematic, but it is not legalistic. It is not satisfied with only the minimum, whatever that minimum might be.

Since it is God who does the "balancing of the books," we cannot accuse Paul of teaching some form of communism. In fact, 2 Corinthians 8:13 is a direct statement against communism. The so-called "communism" of the early church (Acts 2:44-47; 4:32-37) has no relationship to the communistic political and economic systems that are promoted today. The early Christians (like many Christians today) *voluntarily* shared what they had, but did not force people to participate. The entire program was temporary; and the fact that Paul had to take up a special collection to relieve their needs is proof that the program was never meant to be imitated by later generations of Christians.

Grace giving is a matter of faith: we obey God and believe that He will meet our needs as we help to meet the needs of others. As the Jews gathered the manna each day, so we must depend on God to "give us this day our daily bread" (Matt. 6:11). We must not waste or squander what God gives us, neither must we hoard it. In the will of God, it is right to save. (The Jews saved Friday's manna to eat on the Sabbath, and the manna did not decay [Ex. 16:22-26].) But out of God's will, the wealth that we hoard will harm us rather than help us. (See James 5:1-6.)

Beginning in verse 16, Paul suddenly turned from a profound spiritual principle to some practical counsel on how the special collection would be handled. While it is true that grace giving means giving by faith, it is also true that grace giving does not mean giving by chance. The Christian who shares with others must be sure that what he gives is managed honestly and faithfully.

Over the years, I have tried to encourage God's people to support ministries that could be trusted. On more than one occasion, I have warned a church member not to give to an unworthy organization, only to discover that he gave anyway. Then he would come to me a few months later and say, "I sent a check to that outfit, and now I discover that it's a fake!"

"I warned you not to give anything," I would reply very gently.

"Well, the Lord knows my heart," he would argue. "Even though the money was wasted, I got credit for the gift in heaven!"

Grace giving is not foolish giving. Even in a local church, the people who handle the funds must possess certain qualifications. Paul was very careful how he handled money entrusted to him, because he did not want to get the reputation of being a "religious thief." The churches that contributed to the collection chose certain representatives to travel with Paul, so that everything would be done honestly, decently, and in order.

I noted in one of our Sunday School classes in a church I pastored that *one* young man was taking up the offering, counting it, recording it, and then taking it to the Sunday School office. In a nonthreatening way, I suggested that he was putting himself in a dangerous position if anybody accused him of anything, because he could not prove that he was handling the money honestly. "I trust you," I said, "but I don't trust the people who may be watching you and looking for something to criticize." Instead of following my suggestion, he became very angry and left the church.

The men and women in every Christian ministry—a local church, a missionary organization, an evangelistic meeting— should possess the following qualifications if they are to handle God's money.

1. *A God-given desire to serve* (2 Cor. 8:16-17). Paul did not "draft" Titus; the young man had a desire in his heart to assist in the gathering of the special offering. Too often in local churches, men and women are put on the Finance Committee who do not have a sincere desire to serve God in this way. Above all else, a person who handles the Lord's money must have a heart that is right with God.

2. *A burden for lost souls* (2 Cor. 8:18). We do not know who this brother was, but we thank God he had a testimony that he shared the Gospel. Perhaps he was an evangelist; at least he was known to the churches as a man burdened for souls. Local church nominating committees put the good "soul-winners" on the Evangelism Committee or on the Missions Committee, which is fine; but some of them also ought to be on the Finance Committee or the Board of Trustees. Why? *To keep the priorities straight.* I have seen committees approve large sums for buildings and equipment who would

not release funds for a soul-winning ministry.

A discouraged young pastor sought my counsel one day. "My Finance Committee is running scared," he said. "The economic situation has made them so tightfisted, they won't spend any money—and we have a big surplus in the bank!" I had never met his committee, but I knew one thing about them: they needed a burden for lost souls.

3. *A desire to honor God* (2 Cor. 8:19). Too often, financial reports glorify the church, or a group of special donors, and do not glorify God. There is no such thing in the church as "secular and sacred," "business and ministry." All that we do is "sacred business" and ministry for the Lord. When the church constitution says that the deacons (or elders) handle the "spiritual affairs" of the church, and the trustees handle the "material and financial affairs," it is making an unbiblical distinction. *The most spiritual thing a church can do is use its money wisely for spiritual ministry.*

We glorify God by using what He gives us the way He wants it used. If the people who manage church finances are not burdened to glorify God, they will soon be using those funds in ways that dishonor God.

4. *A reputation for honesty* (2 Cor. 8:20-22). Paul made it clear that he welcomed the representatives from the cooperating churches. He wanted to avoid any blame. It is not enough to say, "Well, the Lord sees what we're doing!" We should make certain that *men* can see what we are doing. I like the way J.B. Phillips translates verse 21: "Naturally we want to avoid the slightest breath of criticism in the distribution of their gifts, and to be absolutely aboveboard not only in the sight of God but in the eyes of men."

Personally, I would not support a missionary or Christian worker who was not identified in some way with a reputable committee or board, or a reputable organization. Nor would I give support to any ministry that did not have its books audited and the report available to the donors. I am not saying that all "free-lance" Christian workers are irresponsible; but I would have more confidence in their ministries if they were attached to a board or an organization that supervised their financial support.

Note the emphasis in verse 22 on *diligence*. If there is one quality that is needed when handling finances, it is diligence. I have heard of church treasurers who did not keep up-to-date accurate records of income and expenditures, and who handed in careless annual reports with the excuse that they were "too busy to keep up with the books." Then they should not have taken the office!

5. *A cooperative spirit* (2 Cor. 8:23-24). Titus not only had a heart for this ministry (v. 16), but he knew how to be a good "team member." Paul called him his "partner" and "fellow helper." Titus was not like the committee member I heard about who said at the first meeting, "As long as I am on this committee, there will be no unanimous votes!"

Finance committee members do not *own* the money; it belongs to the Lord. The committee is but a steward, managing the money honestly and carefully for the service of the Lord. Note too that Paul saw the committee as special servants of the *churches*. The raising of this special "relief fund" was a cooperative effort of the Gentile churches, and Paul and the representatives were but "messengers" of the churches. The Greek word is *apostolos*, from which we get "apostle— one sent with a special commission." These dedicated Christians felt an obligation to the churches to do their work honestly and successfully.

Grace giving is an exciting adventure! When you learn to give "by grace, through faith" (just the way you were saved— Eph. 2:8-9), you start to experience a wonderful liberation from things and from circumstances. Instead of *things* possessing you, you start to control them; you develop a new set of values and priorities. You no longer measure life or other people on the basis of money or possessions. If money is the best test of success, then Jesus was a failure, because He was a poor Man!

Grace giving enriches you as you enrich others.

Grace giving makes you more like Jesus Christ.

Have you discovered the thrill of grace giving?

8

The Grace of Giving—Part 2

2 Corinthians 9

It seems strange that we Christians need encouragements to give, when God has given so much to us. God had enriched the Corinthians in a wonderful way, and yet they were hesitant to share what they had with others. They were not accustomed to *grace* giving, so Paul had to explain it to them. Having explained grace giving to them, Paul then tried to motivate them to get involved in the special offering; he did this by sharing five encouragements that relate to grace giving.

Your Giving Will Provoke Others (2 Cor. 9:1-5)
While Christians must not compete with each other in their service for Christ, they ought to "consider one another to provoke unto love and to good works" (Heb. 10:24). When we see what God is doing in and through the lives of others, we ought to strive to serve Him better ourselves. There is a fine line between fleshly imitation and spiritual emulation, and we must be careful in this regard. But a zealous Christian can be the means of stirring up a church and motivating people to

pray, work, witness, and give.

The interesting thing is this: Paul had used the zeal of the Corinthians to challenge the Macedonians; but now he was using the Macedonians to challenge the Corinthians! A year before, the Corinthians had enthusiastically boasted that they would share in the offering, but then they had done nothing. The Macedonians had followed through on their promise, and Paul was afraid that his boasting would be in vain.

Paul sent Titus and the other brothers to Corinth to stir them up to share in the offering. Far more important than the money itself was the spiritual benefit that would come to the church as they shared in response to God's grace in their lives. Paul had written to the church before to tell them how to take up the contributions (1 Cor. 16:1-4), so there was no excuse for their delay. Paul wanted the entire contribution to be ready when he and his "finance committee" arrived, so that there might not be any last-minute collections that might appear to be forced on the church.

What did Paul want to avoid? Embarrassment to himself and to the church if the offering was not ready. For, after all, there were several representatives from the Macedonian churches on the special committee (see Acts 20:4). Paul had boasted to the Macedonians about Corinth, and now he feared that his boasting might be in vain.

Apparently, Paul did not see anything wrong or unspiritual about asking people to promise to give. He did not tell them *how much* they had to promise, but he did expect them to keep their promise. When a person signs up for a telephone, he promises to pay a certain amount each month. If it is acceptable to make financial commitments for things like telephones, cars, and credit cards, certainly it ought to be acceptable to make commitments for the work of the Lord.

Notice the words that Paul used as he wrote about the

collection. It was "ministering to the saints," a service to fellow believers. It was also a "bounty" (2 Cor. 9:5), which means "a generous gift." Was Paul perhaps hinting that the Corinthians give more than they had planned?

However, Paul was careful not to put on any pressure. He wanted their gift to be "a matter of bounty [generosity], and not as of covetousness [something squeezed out of them]." High-pressure offering appeals do not belong to grace giving.

Our greatest encouragement for giving is that it pleases the Lord, but there is nothing wrong with practicing the kind of giving that provokes others to give. This does not mean that we should advertise what we do as individuals, because that kind of practice would violate one of the basic principles of giving: give secretly to the Lord (Matt. 6:1-4). However, Paul was writing to *churches;* and it is not wrong for congregations to announce what they have given collectively. If our motive is to boast, then we are not practicing grace giving. But if our desire is to provoke others to share, then God's grace can work through us to help others.

Your Giving Will Bless You (2 Cor. 9:6-11)

"Give, and it shall be given unto you," was our Lord's promise; and it still holds true (Luke 6:38). The "good measure" He gives back to us is not always money or material goods, but it is always worth far more than we gave. Giving is not something we *do*, but something we *are*. Giving is a way of life for the Christian who understands the grace of God. The world simply does not understand a statement like Proverbs 11:24: "There is that scattereth, and yet increaseth; and there is that withholdeth more than is meet, but it tendeth to poverty." In grace giving, our motive is not "to get something," but receiving God's blessing is one of the fringe benefits.

If our giving is to bless us and build us up, we must be

careful to follow the principles that Paul explained in this section.

1. *The principle of increase: we reap in measure as we sow* (2 Cor. 9:6). This principle needs little explanation, because we see it operating in everyday life. The farmer who sows much seed will have a better chance for a bigger harvest. The investor who puts a large sum of money in the bank will certainly collect more dividends. The more we invest in the work of the Lord, the more "fruit" will abound to our account (Phil. 4:10-20).

Whenever we are tempted to forget this principle, we need to remind ourselves that God was unsparing in His giving. "He that spared not His own Son, but delivered Him up for us all, how shall He not with Him also freely give us all things?" (Rom. 8:32) In both nature and grace, God is a generous Giver; and he who would be godly must follow the divine example.

2. *The principle of intent: we reap as we sow with right motives* (2 Cor. 9:7). Motive makes absolutely no difference to the farmer! If he sows good seed and has good weather, he will reap a harvest whether he is working for profit, pleasure, or pride. It makes no difference how he plans to use the money that he earns, the harvest will probably come just the same.

But not so with the Christian: motive in giving (or in any other activity) is vitally important. Our giving must come from the heart, and the motive in the heart must please God. We must not be "sad givers" who give grudgingly, or "mad givers" who give because we have to ("of necessity"); but we should be "glad givers" who cheerfully share what we have because we have experienced the grace of God. "He that hath a bountiful eye shall be blessed" (Prov. 22:9).

If we cannot give joyfully (the Greek word gives us our

English word *hilarious*), then we must open our hearts to the Lord and ask Him to grant us His grace. Certainly God can bless a gift that is given out of a sense of duty, but God cannot bless the giver unless his heart is right. Grace giving means that God blesses the giver as well as the gift, and that the giver is a blessing to others.

3. *The principle of immediacy: we reap even while we are sowing* (2 Cor. 9:8-11). The farmer has to wait for his harvest, but the believer who practices grace giving begins to reap the harvest immediately. To be sure, there are long-range benefits from our giving, but there are also immediate blessings.

To begin with, we start to share God's abundant grace (v. 8). The "universals" in this verse are staggering: *all* grace; *always*; *all* sufficiency; *every* good work. This does not mean that God makes every Christian wealthy in material things; but it does mean that the Christian who practices grace giving will always have what he needs when he needs it. Furthermore, the grace of God enriches him morally and spiritually so that he grows in Christian character. In his walk and his work, he depends wholly on the sufficiency of God.

It is disturbing to see how many Christians today are totally dependent on others for their spiritual resources. Preachers cannot get sermons unless they borrow them from a book or a cassette. Church officers are bewildered about what to do with a problem unless they phone two or three well-known preachers for advice. Far too many church members have to consult with the pastor once a week or they fall apart spiritually.

The word *sufficiency* means "adequate resources within" (see Phil. 4:11). Through Jesus Christ, we can have the adequacy we need to meet the demands of life. As Christians, we do need to help and encourage one another; but we must not depend on one another. Our dependence must be on the Lord.

He alone can give us that "well of water" in the heart that makes us sufficient for life (John 4:14).

We not only share God's grace, but we also share His righteousness (2 Cor. 9:9). Paul quoted Psalm 112:9 to prove his point. That psalm describes the righteous man who has no fears because his heart is sincere and obedient to the Lord. Paul did not suggest that we *earn* righteousness by our giving, because the only way to get righteousness is by faith in Jesus Christ. However, if our hearts are right, our giving will be used by God to make our characters righteous. Grace giving builds Christian character.

We reap as we sow, and we share God's miracle multiplication of what we give and do (2 Cor. 9:10). The farmer has to decide how much seed he will keep for food, and how much he will plant. If the harvest has been lean, there is less seed available both for eating and planting. But the Christian who believes in grace giving never has to worry about this decision: God supplies all that he needs. There is always spiritual and material "bread" for the eating and spiritual and material "seed" for the sowing.

Paul referred here to Isaiah 55:10-11, a passage that uses "seed" and "bread" to refer to both the Word of God and to the literal harvest in the field. There is no such thing as "secular" and "sacred" in the Christian life. The giving of money is just as spiritual an act as the singing of a hymn or the handing out of a Gospel tract. *Money is seed.* If we give it according to the principles of grace, it will multiply to the glory of God and meet many needs. If we use it in ways other than God desires, the harvest will be poor.

Finally, as we sow, we are enriched and we enrich others (2 Cor. 9:11). The farmer reaps immediate physical benefits as he works in his field, but he has to wait for the harvest. The Christian who is motivated by grace reaps the blessings of personal enrichment in his or her own life and character, and this enrichment benefits others. The final result is glory to God as others give thanks to Him. Paul was careful to point out that grace giving does not bring credit to us; it brings thanksgiving to God. We are but channels through whom God works to meet the needs of others.

But verse 11 teaches another truth: God enriches us so that we may give even more bountifully. One of the joys of grace giving is the joy of giving more and more. Everything we have—not just our income—belongs to God, is given to God, and is used by God to accomplish His work. We are enriched in everything because we share everything with Him and with others.

As a pastor, I have watched young Christians lay hold of these principles of grace giving and start to grow. It has been a great joy to see them trust God as their giving is motivated by grace. At the same time, I have seen other believers smile at these principles and gradually impoverish themselves. Some of them "prospered" financially, but their income was their downfall: it did not enrich them. They had their reward, but they lost their opportunities for spiritual enrichment.

Grace giving means that we really believe that God is the great giver, and we use our material and spiritual resources accordingly. You simply cannot outgive God!

Your Giving Will Meet Needs (2 Cor. 9:12)
Paul introduced a new word for the offering: *service.* It means "priestly service," so once again, Paul lifted the offering to the highest level possible. He saw this collection as a "spiritual sacrifice" presented to God, the way a priest presents a costly sacrifice on the altar.

Christians no longer bring animals as sacrifices to God, because the work of Christ on the cross has ended the levitical system (Heb. 10:1-14). But the material gifts we bring to the Lord become "spiritual sacrifices," if they are given in the name of Jesus (1 Peter 2:5; Heb. 13:15-16; Phil. 4:10-20).

But the emphasis in 2 Corinthians 9:12 is on the fact that their offering would meet the needs of poor saints in Judea. "For the administration of this service not only supplieth the want of the saints, but is abundant also by many thanksgivings unto God" (v. 12). The Gentile believers could have given a number of excuses for not giving. "It's not our fault that they had a famine and are poor!" might have been one of them. Or, "The churches closer to Judea ought to give them help." Or, "We believe in giving, but we think we should first take care of our own."

When a Christian starts to think of excuses for not giving, he automatically moves out of the sphere of grace giving. *Grace never looks for a reason; it only looks for an opportunity.* If there is a need to be met, the grace-controlled Christian will do what he can to meet it.

"As we have therefore opportunity, let us do good unto all men, especially unto them who are of the household of faith" (Gal. 6:10). Paul admonished the wealthy Christians "that they do good, that they be rich in good works, ready to distribute, willing to communicate [share]" (1 Tim. 6:18). Most of us would not consider ourselves "wealthy," but the rest of the world does.

However, *we* are not the ones who get the glory; it is the Lord who is glorified (Matt. 5:16). Many people will give thanksgiving to God because of our sharing in the meeting of their needs. We may not hear that thanksgiving on earth today, but we will hear it in heaven when the church is gathered together.

It might be profitable here to notice Paul's use of the concept of *abundance* as he wrote this letter. He opened the letter with abundant suffering that was matched by abundant comfort (2 Cor. 1:5). He also mentioned abundant grace (4:15) and abundant joy and liberality (8:2). Because of God's abundant grace, we can abound always in every good work (9:8). The apostle saw the Christian life as one of abundance, for Jesus Christ can make us adequate for every situation.

Our giving ought to provide for necessities, not subsidize luxuries. There are needs to be met and our limited resources must not be squandered. While it is true that the need itself is not the only reason for giving, for there are always more needs than any one Christian or church can meet; but the need is important. Some needs are greater than others, and some needs are more strategic than others. We need accurate information as well as spiritual illumination as we seek to meet the many needs that are pressing upon us today.

Your Giving Will Glorify God (2 Cor. 9:13)

"Let your light so shine before men," said our Lord, "that they may see your good works, and glorify your Father which is in heaven" (Matt. 5:16). This is one of the beauties of church giving: no individual gets the glory that belongs only to God.

For what would the grateful Jewish believers give thanks? Of course, they would praise God for the generosity of the Gentile churches in meeting their physical and material needs. But they would also praise God for the spiritual submission of the Gentiles, their obedience to the Spirit of God who gave them the desire to give. They would say, "Those Gentiles not only preach the Gospel, but they also practice it!"

The little phrase *and unto all men* at the end of this verse (2 Cor. 9:13) is significant. The Jewish believers would give thanks that *others* were also being assisted by the Gentile churches. Each little congregation that received aid would be thankful for that aid and for the aid being given to others.

Instead of saying, "Why didn't *we* get more?" they would be praising God that others in need were also being helped. That is the way grace giving works.

It might be good for our churches to take inventory to see if anybody is giving thanks to God for our obedience and generosity. No amount of evangelistic zeal or worship activity can compensate for lost opportunities in serving others and meeting their practical needs. It is not a matter of choosing one and ignoring the other. There must be a balance of sharing the Gospel and meeting practical needs, if our light is to shine brightly and steadily. It has well been said that it is difficult to preach the Gospel to a hungry man. (See James 2:15-16.)

I recall reading about a wealthy Christian who daily, at family devotions, prayed for the needs of the missionaries that his church supported. One morning, after he had concluded family prayers, his little boy said, "Dad, if I had your check-book, I could answer your prayers!" A discerning lad, indeed!

Your Giving Will Unite God's People (2 Cor. 9:14-15)

This, of course, was one of the major purposes that Paul had on his heart when he challenged the Gentile churches to assist the Jewish believers. The extreme legalists in the church had accused Paul of being anti-Jewish and even anti-Law. The Gentile churches were removed from the "mother church" in Jerusalem both by distance and culture. Paul wanted to prevent a division in the church, and the "relief offering" was a part of that prevention program.

In what ways would this offering bind the Jewish and Gentile congregations more closely? For one thing, the offering was an expression of love. The Gentiles were not obligated to share (though Paul did see the offering as the payment of a "spiritual debt," Rom. 15:25-27), but they did so because of the grace of God. The Jews, in turn, would feel themselves bound to their Gentile brothers and sisters.

Another spiritual bond would be prayer. "And in their prayers for you their hearts will go out to you, because of the surpassing grace God has given you" (2 Cor. 9:14, NIV). Were the Gentile churches "buying" the prayer support of the Jewish churches? Not in the least! Paul envisioned a spontaneous expression of love, praise, and prayer as he shared the offering in Judea.

I have had the experience of visiting several mission fields and hearing believers there say, "We are praying for you." I recall chatting with a fine Christian from eastern Europe, who said, "We are praying for you in the United States, because in some ways, you have a more difficult time being spiritual Christians than we do." When I asked him to explain, he smiled and said, "You have relatively easy lives, and comfort is an enemy of the spiritual life. In eastern Europe, we know who our enemies are, and we know who our friends are. Where you live, it is easy to be fooled. Yes, we are praying for you!"

Both the Jewish and the Gentile churches would be drawn closer to Jesus Christ. "Thanks [grace] be unto God for His unspeakable [indescribable] gift" (v. 15). In Jesus Christ, all human distinctions are erased, and we no longer see each other as Jews or Gentiles, rich or poor, givers or recipients. "For ye are all one in Christ Jesus" (Gal. 3:28).

It is sad when our giving becomes a substitute for our living. A church officer once complained to me, "I'll give any amount of money you want for missions. Just don't make me listen to a missionary speak!" When a Christian practices grace giving, his money is not a substitute for either his concern or his service. He first gives himself to the Lord (2 Cor. 8:5) and then he gives what he has. His gift is a symbol, as it were, of the surrender of his heart. You cannot separate the gift and the giver when your giving is motivated by God's grace.

I suggest you read 2 Corinthians 8 and 9 again, and that you note the emphasis on the grace of God. If our churches and other ministries would get back to grace giving, there would be fewer high-pressure offering appeals, fewer gimmicks to raise funds, and fewer complaints from the people of God. Instead, there would be plenty of money available for the ministries that truly magnify the grace of God. And I think that the unsaved people in the world would sit up and take notice!

You and I are saved because God believed in grace giving. How much do *we* believe in grace giving?

9

Ministerial Misunderstandings

2 Corinthians 10

Whenever I receive a critical letter from a reader or a radio listener, I usually set it aside in a special file until I feel I am really ready to answer it. On a few occasions, I have replied to letters too quickly, and I have regretted it. By waiting, I give myself time to think and pray, to "read between the lines," and to prepare a reply that would do the most good and the least damage.

The Spirit led Paul to use a wise approach as he wrote to the Corinthians. He was writing to a divided church (1 Cor. 1:11ff), a church that was resisting his authority, and a church that was being seduced by false teachers. So, first he explained his ministry so that they would no longer doubt his sincerity. He then encouraged them to share in the offering, for he knew that this challenge would help them grow in their spiritual lives. Grace giving and grace living go together.

Now, in the last section of the letter, Paul challenged the rebels in the church—including the false teachers—and enforced his apostolic ministry. As you read chapters 10—13, you will find Paul referring directly to his accusers (10:7, 10-12; 11:4, 20-23, for example) and answering their false charges. He does not hide the fact that the Judaizers in the church are ministers of Satan who want to destroy the work of God (11:12-15).

Paul used one word 20 times in chapters 10—13, the word translated *boast* or *glory.* When you first read these chapters, you get the impression that Paul was bragging about himself; but such was not the case. Paul "gloried in Jesus Christ" and not in himself or his achievements (Rom. 5:11; Gal. 6:14; Phil. 3:3). He boasted to others about the Corinthians, but it seemed that his boasting might be in vain (2 Cor. 7:4, 14; 8:24).

Keep in mind that Paul was not defending himself personally; he was defending his ministry and his apostolic authority. He was not involved in a "personality contest" with other ministers. His enemies did not hesitate to accuse him falsely, nor did they hesitate to promote themselves (11:12). It was the worldly attitude of the Corinthians that *forced* Paul to defend himself by reminding them of his life and ministry. Paul never hesitated to talk about Jesus Christ, but he did refuse to talk about himself, unless there was good reason to do so.

Finally, when Paul did *boast,* he limited himself to the ministry God had given him (10:13), and then he emphasized his *sufferings,* not his successes. When this letter was read in the Corinthian assembly, it must have brought shame to the hearts of those who had criticized Paul—and it must have made the Judaizers look foolish.

Paul's first step in enforcing his ministry was to correct the misunderstandings that existed in the minds of the people with reference to his work. They did not understand three important areas of ministry.

How to Wage Spiritual Warfare (2 Cor. 10:1-6)

1. The accusation (2 Cor. 10:1-2) is not difficult to find. The rebels in the church (led by the Judaizers) said that Paul was very courageous when he wrote letters from a distance, but very timid and even weak when he was present with the Corinthians. (See also vv. 9-11.) The Judaizers, of course, were consistently overbearing in their attitudes—and the people loved them (11:20). Paul's "inconsistent" manner of life paralleled his "yes and no" approach to making promises (1:15-20).

When Paul founded the church at Corinth, his purpose was to exalt Christ and not himself (1 Cor. 2:1-5). Christians usually grow the way they are born. If they are born in an atmosphere of dictatorial leadership, they grow up depending on man's wisdom and strength. If they are born in an atmosphere of humility and love, they learn to depend on the Lord. Paul wanted his converts to trust the Lord, and not the servant; so he deliberately "played down" his own authority and ability.

How ignorant the Corinthians were, even after all that Paul had taught them. They failed to realize that true spiritual power is in "meekness and gentleness" (2 Cor. 10:1), not in "throwing weight around." Paul's very attitude in these opening verses disarmed his opponents. (In fact, his use of his own name is significant; for *Paul* means "little.") If Paul was a weakling, then so was Jesus Christ; for Jesus exhibited meekness and gentleness (Matt. 11:29). However, our Lord could also be stern and even angry when the occasion demanded it. (See Matt. 15:1-2; 23:13-33; Mark 11:15-17; John 2:13-16.) Paul was warning them in a loving way, "Please don't force me to come and show how bold I can be!"

2. The answer (2 Cor. 10:3-6) reveals what spiritual warfare is all about. Because the Corinthians (led by the false teachers) judged Paul's ministry by the outward appearance, they completely missed the power that was there. They were evaluating things "according to the flesh" (v. 2) and not according to the Spirit. The Judaizers, like some "great religious personalities" today, impressed the people with their overpowering abilities, their oratorical powers, and their "commendations" from church leaders.

Paul took a different approach; for, though he was as human as anyone else, he did not depend on the human but on the divine, the spiritual weapons provided by the Lord. His warfare was not according to the flesh, because he was not fighting against flesh and blood (see Eph. 6:10ff). You cannot fight spiritual battles with carnal weapons.

The word *warfare* in verse 4 means "campaign." Paul was not simply fighting a little skirmish in Corinth; the attack of the enemy there was part of a large satanic campaign. The powers of hell are still trying to destroy the work of God (Matt. 16:18), and it is important that we not yield any ground to the enemy, not even one church!

There are walls of resistance in the minds of people, and these walls (like the walls of Jericho) must be pulled down. What are these "mental walls"? Reasonings that are opposed to the truth of God's Word. Pride of intelligence that exalts itself. Paul was not attacking intelligence, but intellectualism, the high-minded attitude that makes people think they know more than they really do (Rom. 12:16). Paul had faced this "wisdom of men" when he founded the church (1 Cor. 1:18ff), and it had surfaced again with the coming of the Judaizers.

Paul's attitude of humility was actually one of his strongest weapons, for pride plays right into the hands of Satan. The meek Son of God had far more power than Pilate (see John 19:11), and He proved it. Paul used spiritual weapons to tear down the opposition—prayer, the Word of God; love, the power of the Spirit at work in his life. He did not depend on personality, human abilities, or even the authority he had as an apostle. However, he was ready to punish the offenders, if necessary, once the congregation had submitted to the Lord.

Many believers today do not realize that the church is involved in warfare, and those who do understand the seriousness of the Christian battle do not always know how to fight the battle. They try to use human methods to defeat demonic forces, and these methods are doomed to fail. When Joshua and his army marched around Jericho for a week, the spectators thought they were mad. When the Jews trusted God and obeyed orders, they brought down the high walls and conquered the enemy (Josh. 6:1-20).

When I was pastoring in Chicago, I met weekly with three pastor friends, and together we united in "warfare praying." We claimed God's promise to cast down the wrong thinking that was keeping people from surrendering to God; and God did great things in the lives of many people for whom we interceded. Once the walls in the mind have been torn down, the door to the heart can be opened.

How to Use Spiritual Authority (2 Cor. 10:7-11)

One of the most difficult lessons Christ's disciples had to learn was that, in the kingdom of God, position and power were no evidence of authority. Jesus warned His followers not to pattern their leadership after that of the Gentiles who loved to "lord it over" others and to act important. (See Mark 10:35-45.) The example we must follow is that of Jesus Christ who came as a servant and ministered to others. Paul followed that example.

But the Corinthians were not spiritually minded enough to discern what Paul was doing. They contrasted his meekness with the "personality power" of the Judaizers, and they concluded that Paul had no authority at all. To be sure, he wrote powerful letters; but his physical appearance was weak, and his speech "unimpressive." They were judging by the outward appearance and were not exercising spiritual discernment.

Some friends and I once listened to a man preach whose entire sermon was made up of impressive "big words," an occasional quotation from the Bible (usually taken out of context), and many references to world events and "the signs of the times." As we left the meeting, one of my friends said, "First Kings 19:11 describes that performance perfectly: 'The Lord was not in the wind.' " Yet people around us were saying that it was "the most wonderful sermon" they had ever heard. I seriously doubt that 10 minutes later, they were able to recall one concrete thing that the preacher had said.

Paul did not deny that he had authority, but he did refuse to exercise that authority in an unspiritual manner. The purpose for his authority was to build them up, not tear them down; and it requires much more skill to build than to destroy. Furthermore, it takes love to build up (1 Cor. 8:1); and the Corinthians interpreted Paul's love and meekness as a sign of weakness.

The difference between Paul and the Judaizers was this: Paul used his authority to build up the church, while the Judaizers used the church to build up their authority.

In my many years of pastoral and itinerant ministry, I have never ceased to be amazed at how some local churches treat their pastors. If a man shows love and true humility, they resist his leadership and break his heart. The next pastor will be a "dictator" who "runs the church"—and he gets just what he wants. And the people love him and brag about him! Our Lord was treated the same way, so perhaps we should not be surprised.

The opponents in the church were accusing Paul of not

being a true apostle; for, if he were a true apostle, he would show it by using his authority. On the other hand, if Paul *had* "thrown his weight around," they would have found fault with that. No matter what course Paul took, they were bound to condemn him. This is what always happens when church members are not spiritually minded, but evaluate ministry from a worldly viewpoint.

But their accusation backfired. If Paul was not an apostle, then he was a counterfeit and not even a believer. But if that were true, then the church at Corinth was not a true church. Paul had already made it clear that nobody could separate his ministry and his personal life (2 Cor. 1:12-14). If he were a deceiver, then the Corinthians were the deceived!

Paul also pointed out that there was no contradiction between his preaching and his writing. He was bold in his letters because that was what was needed at the time. How much more would he have enjoyed being able to write with gentleness. But it would not have achieved the desired purpose. And, even when he wrote "weighty and powerful" letters, he wrote from a heart of love. "You had better prepare for my next visit," he was saying, "because if it is necessary, I will show you how powerful I can be."

How a Christian uses authority is an evidence of his spiritual maturity and character. An immature person *swells* as he uses his authority, but a mature person *grows* in the use of authority, and others grow with him. The wise pastor, like the wise parent, knows when to wait in loving patience and when to act with determined power. It takes more power to wait than to strike. A mature person does not use authority to *demand* respect, but to *command* respect. Mature leaders suffer while they wait to act, while immature leaders act impetuously and make others suffer.

The false teachers depended on "letters of recommendation" for their authority, but Paul had a divine commission from heaven. The life that he lived and the work that he did were "credentials" enough, for it was evident that the hand of God was upon his life. Paul could dare to write, "From henceforth let no man trouble me; for I bear in my body the marks of the Lord Jesus" (Gal. 6:17).

When my wife and I have ministered in England, we have always tried to arrange our schedule so that we might visit in London. We especially enjoy shopping in Selfridge's and Harrod's, London's two leading department stores. H. Gordon Selfridge, who built the great store that bears his name, always claimed that he was a success because he was a leader and not a "boss." The leader says "Let's go!" while the boss says "Go!" The boss *knows* how it is done, but the leader *shows* how it is done. The boss inspires fear; the leader inspires enthusiasm based on respect and good will. The boss fixes the *blame* for the breakdown, while the true leader fixes the breakdown. The boss keeps saying "I" while the leader says "We." Mr. Selfridge's philosophy of management would certainly agree with the Apostle Paul's philosophy of leadership.

How to Measure Spiritual Ministry (2 Cor. 10:12-18)

I suppose more problems have been caused by people "measuring the ministry" than by any other activity in the church. If the work of the church is the work of God, and if the work of God is a miracle, how do we go about measuring a miracle? In His personal examination of the seven churches named in Revelation 2—3, the Lord Jesus measured them far differently than they measured themselves. The church that thought it was poor, He considered to be rich; and the church that boasted of its wealth, He declared to be poor (2:8-11; 3:14-22).

Some people measure ministry only by statistics. While it is true that the early church did take note of numbers (Acts 2:41; 4:4), it is also true that uniting with the church at that time was a much more difficult (and dangerous) thing (see Acts 5:13). Some years ago, one of America's large denominations had as its theme, "A Million More in '64, and Every One a Tither!" I heard one of their leading preachers comment, "If we get a million more like the last million, God help us!" Quantity is no guarantee of quality.

1. *False measurement* (2 Cor. 10:12). The Judaizers were great on measuring their ministry, because a religion of external activities is much easier to measure than one of internal transformation. The legalist can measure what he does and what he does not do, but the Lord is the only one who can see spiritual growth in a believer's heart. Sometimes those who are growing the most feel like they are less than the least.

In a sense, the Judaizers belonged to a "mutual admiration society" that set up its own standards and measured everybody by them. Of course, those inside the group were successful; those outside were failures. Paul was one of the outsiders, so he was considered a failure. Unfortunately, they did not measure themselves by Jesus Christ (see Eph. 4:12-16). If they had, it would have made a difference.

2. *True measurement* (2 Cor. 10:13-18). Paul suggests three questions we may ask ourselves as we seek to measure our ministries by the will of God.

Am I where God wants me to be? (vv. 13-14) God "assigned a field" in which Paul was to work: he was the apostle to the Gentiles (Acts 9:15; 22:21; Eph. 3). He was also to go where no other apostle had ministered; he was to be a "pioneer preacher" to the Gentiles.

Paul used a bit of "sanctified sarcasm" in his defense. "The area God assigned to me included even you Corinthians!" (See

2 Cor. 10:13.) It was not the Judaizers who had come to Corinth with the Gospel. They, like the cultists today, arrived on the scene only after the church had already been established. (See Rom. 15:15-22.)

Churches and ministers are not competing with each other; they are competing with themselves. God is not going to measure us on the basis of the gifts and opportunities that He gave to Charles Spurgeon or Billy Sunday. He will measure my work by what He assigned to me. God requires faithfulness above everything else (1 Cor. 4:2).

There is something intimidating about attending a pastors' conference or a denominational convention, because the people on the program are usually the "front-runners" with the best records. Young pastors and older men in narrow places often go home carrying feelings of guilt because their faithful work does not seem to produce as much fruit. Some of these discouraged men then try all kinds of programs and promotions, only to have more disappointment; and then they contemplate leaving the ministry. If only they would realize that God measures their ministries on the basis of where He has put them, and not on the basis of what is going on in some other city, it would encourage them to stay on the job and keep being faithful.

Is God glorified by my ministry? (2 Cor. 10:15-17) This is another jibe at the Judaizers who stole other men's converts and claimed them as their own. Paul would not boast about another man's work, nor would he invade another man's territory. Whatever work he did, God did through him, and God alone should receive the glory.

I once listened to a man give a lecture on how to build a large Sunday School. Everything in the lecture was correct and certainly had worked in some of the large ministries in the United States. The only problem was, *the man had never built a large Sunday School himself!* He had visited many of the large ministries, interviewed the pastors and staff members, and developed his lecture. After he finished his lecture, people flocked to his side to ask questions and get autographs. I happened to be standing next to a pastor who had built one of the finest churches—and one of the largest—in America.

"Those people ought to be talking to you," I said to him. "You've done it and you know more about Sunday School work than he does!"

"Let him enjoy himself," said my friend with a kind smile. "We're all doing the same work, and all that counts is that God is glorified."

Paul added another bit of "holy irony" when he told the Corinthians that the only thing that had kept him from going to "the regions beyond" them was their own lack of faith. Had they been submissive to his leadership and obedient to the Word, he could have reached other lost souls; but they created so many problems for him, that he had to take time from missionary evangelism to solve the problems in the church. "I would have better statistics to report," he was saying, "but you hindered me."

Paul quoted Jeremiah 9:24 in verse 17, a statement he had also quoted in 1 Corinthians 1:31. The Corinthians were prone to glory in men, especially now that the Judaizers had taken over in the church. When the Corinthians heard the "reports" of what these teachers had done, and when they saw the "letters of recommendation" that they carried, the church was quite carried away with them. As a result, Paul and his ministry looked small and unsuccessful.

But the final test is not when the reports are published for the annual meeting. The final test comes at the Judgment Seat of Christ, "and then shall every man have praise of God" (1 Cor. 4:5). If men get the glory, then God cannot be glorified.

"I am the Lord: that is My name: and My glory will I not give to another" (Isa. 42:8).

This is not to suggest that well-known ministers with flourishing works are robbing God of glory. As we grow and bear "much fruit," we bring glory to the Father (John 15:1-8). But we must be careful that it is "fruit" that comes from spiritual life and not "results" that appear when we manipulate people and manufacture statistics.

Can the Lord commend my work? (2 Cor. 10:18) We may commend ourselves or be commended by others, and still not deserve the commendation of God. How does God approve our work? By testing it. The word *approved* in verse 18 means "to approve by testing." There is a future testing at the Judgment Seat of Christ (1 Cor. 3:10ff), but there is also a present testing of the work that we do. God permits difficulties to come to local churches in order that the work might be tested and approved.

Over the years, I have seen ministries tested by financial losses, the invasion of false doctrine, the emergence of proud leaders who want to "run the church," and the challenge of change. Some of the churches have fallen apart and almost died, because the work was not spiritual. Other ministries have grown because of the trials and have become purer and stronger; and, through it all, God was glorified.

Certainly our ministries must keep records and issue reports, but we must not fall into the "snare of statistics" and think that numbers are the only measurement of ministry. Each situation is unique, and no ministry can honestly be evaluated on the basis of some other ministry. The important thing is that we are where God wants us to be, doing what He wants us to do so that He might be glorified. Motive is as much a part of God's measurement of our work as is growth. If we are seeking to glorify and please God alone, and if we are not afraid of His evaluation of our hearts and lives, then we need not fear the estimates of men or their criticisms.

"But he that glorieth, let him glory in the Lord" (v. 17).

10

Father Knows Best

2 Corinthians 11

If you were a Christian minister, how would you go about convincing the people in your congregation that you really loved them?

This was the problem Paul faced as he wrote this epistle. If he reminded the people of the work he did among them, they would only reply, "Paul is bragging!" If he said nothing about his ministry at Corinth, the Judaizers would say, "See, we told you Paul didn't accomplish anything!"

So what did Paul do? He was led by the Spirit of God to use a beautiful image—a comparison—that was certain to reach the hearts of the believers at Corinth. He compared himself to a "spiritual father" caring for his family. He had used this image before to remind the Corinthians that, as a "father" he had begotten them through the Gospel, and that he could discipline them if he felt it was necessary (1 Cor. 4:14-21). They were his beloved spiritual children, and he wanted the very best for them.

Paul gave them three evidences of his fatherly love for them.

His Jealousy over the Church (2 Cor. 11:1-6, 13-15)

True love is never envious, but it has a right to be jealous over those who are loved. A husband is jealous over his wife and rightfully resents and resists any rivalry that threatens their love for each other. A true patriot has every right to be jealous over his freedom and will fight to protect it. Likewise, a father (or a mother) is jealous over his children and seeks to protect them from anything that will harm them.

The *picture* here is that of a loving father who has a daughter engaged to be married. He feels it is his privilege and duty to keep her pure, so that he can present her to her husband with joy and not with sorrow. Paul saw the local church as a bride, engaged to be married to Jesus Christ. (See Eph. 5:22ff and Rom. 7:4.) That marriage will not take place until Jesus Christ has come for His bride (Rev. 19:1-9). Meanwhile, the church—and this means individual Christians— must keep herself pure as she prepares to meet her Beloved.

The *peril*, then, is that of unfaithfulness to her fiancé. The engaged woman owes her love and allegiance to but one—her betrothed. If she shares herself with any other man, she is guilty of unfaithfulness. The word translated *simplicity* in 2 Corinthians 11:3 means "sincerity, singleness of devotion." A divided heart leads to a defiled life and a destroyed relationship.

The image of love and marriage, and the need for faithfulness, is often used in the Bible. The Prophet Jeremiah saw the people of Judah losing their love for God, and he warned them. "Thus saith the Lord; 'I remember thee, the kindness of thy youth, the love of thine espousals' " (Jer. 2:2). The nation of Judah had lost its "honeymoon love" and was guilty of worshiping idols. Jesus used the same image when He warned the church at Ephesus: "Nevertheless I have somewhat against thee, because thou hast left thy first love" (Rev. 2:4).

The *person behind the peril* was Satan, pictured here as the serpent. The reference is to Genesis 3. It is worth noting that Paul had a great deal to say about our adversary, the devil, when he wrote this letter to the Corinthians. He warned that Satan had several devices for attacking believers. He can burden the consciences of believers who have sinned (2 Cor. 2:10-11), blind the minds of unbelievers (4:4) or beguile the minds of believers (11:3), and even buffet the bodies of God's ministers (12:7).

The focus here is on the mind, for Satan is a liar and tries to get us to listen to his lies, ponder them, and then believe them. This is what he did with Eve. First, he *questioned* God's word ("Yea, hath God said . . . ?"), then he *denied* God's word ("Ye shall not surely die!"), and then he *substituted his own lie* ("Ye shall be as gods . . . ") (Gen. 3:1, 4-5).

Satan, of course, is crafty. He knows that believers will not immediately accept a lie, so the enemy has to "bait the hook" and make it easy for us to accept what he has to offer. Basically, Satan is an imitator: he copies what God does and then tries to convince us that his offer is better than God's. How does he do this? By using counterfeit ministers who pretend to serve God, but who are really the servants of Satan.

Satan has a counterfeit gospel (Gal. 1:6-12) that involves a different saviour and a different spirit. Unfortunately, the Corinthians had "welcomed" this "new gospel," which was a mixture of law and grace and not a true gospel at all. There is only one Gospel, and therefore there can be only one Saviour (1 Cor. 15:1ff). When you trust the Saviour, you receive the Holy Spirit of God within, and there is only one Holy Spirit.

The *preachers* of this false Gospel (and they are with us yet today) are described in 2 Corinthians 11:13-15. They claimed to have divine authority as God's servants, but their authority was bogus. They claimed that the true servants of God were all imposters; in Paul's day, they said this about him. They even claimed to be "super-apostles," on a much higher level than Paul. With their clever oratory, they mesmerized the ignorant believers, while at the same time they pointed out that Paul was not a very gifted speaker (v. 6; 10:10). How tragic it is when unstable believers are swayed by the "fair speech" of Satan's ministers, instead of standing firm on the basic truths of the Gospel taught to them by faithful pastors and teachers.

"They are not 'super-apostles' at all!" warned Paul. "They are *pseudo* apostles—false apostles!" Their motive is not to glorify God, but to get personal gain by capturing converts. Their methods are deceitful (2:17; 4:2). The basic idea here is that of using bait to catch fish. They offer church members a Christian life that is "superior" to that described in the New Testament, a life that is an unbiblical mixture of law and grace.

Instead of being empowered by the Spirit, these ministers are energized by Satan. Three times, Paul used the word *transform* in referring to their work (see 11:13, 14, 15). This Greek word simply means "to disguise, to masquerade." There is a change on the outside, but there is no change on the inside. Satan's workers, like Satan himself, never appear in their true character; they always wear a disguise and hide behind a mask.

As I was writing this book, several of Satan's "masquerading ministers" appeared at my front door. One of them, an attractive young lady, tried to tell me she was working for world peace; but when I confronted her, she admitted that she belonged to a cult. Two well-dressed young men introduced themselves with, "We are here representing Jesus Christ!" I quickly informed them that I knew what group they represented, and I closed the door. I did not even say "Good-bye." If you think I was unkind, read 2 John 5-11—and obey it.

Paul proved his love for the church by protecting it from the attacks of false teachers; and yet the members of the church "fell for" the Judaizers and let them come in. The Corinthians had "left their first love" and were no longer giving single-hearted devotion to Jesus Christ. It was not only that they had turned against Paul, but they had turned away from Christ; and that was far more serious.

His Generosity to the Church (2 Cor. 11:7-12)

A loving parent provides for the needs of the family, and Paul sacrificed that he might minister to the church at Corinth. While Paul was there, he labored with his own hands as a tentmaker (Acts 18:1-3) and even received gifts from other churches so that he might evangelize Corinth. In other words, it had cost the Corinthians nothing to benefit from the apostolic ministry of this great man of God.

Did the Corinthians appreciate the sacrifices that Paul made for them? No, most of them did not. In fact, the Judaizers even used Paul's financial policy as "proof" that he was not a true apostle. After all, if he *were* a true apostle, he would accept financial support.

Paul had already explained his policy in a previous letter (1 Cor. 9). He had pointed out that he *was* a true apostle because he had seen the risen Christ and had been commissioned by Him. Paul had the right to ask for financial support, just as God's faithful servants do today; but he had deliberately given up that right so that nobody could accuse him of using the Gospel simply as a means of making money. He gave up his "financial rights" for the Gospel's sake and for the sake of lost sinners who might stumble over anything that gave the impression of being "religious business."

On the other hand, it was the Judaizers who were guilty of

"peddling the Gospel" for personal profit. Paul had preached the Gospel to them *freely* (2 Cor. 11:7, literally "without charge, for nothing"), but the false teachers were preaching a *false* gospel—and robbing the church (v. 20). Paul used a bit of irony in verse 8: "Yes, I have been a 'robber.' I 'robbed' other churches so I would not have to 'rob' you!" And now the Judaizers were *really* robbing them.

A loving father does not lay his burdens on his children. Instead, he sacrifices so that the children might have what they need. It is a difficult thing to teach children the difference between "prices" and "values." Children seem to have no idea what it means for parents to go to work and earn the money that provides what the family needs. When one of my nephews was very young, he heard his parents discussing the purchase of some major appliance, and he could not understand why they did not just go out and buy it. "Why don't you just write one of those pieces of paper?" he asked, pointing to his father's checkbook. He did not understand that there has to be money in the bank to back up what you write on those "pieces of paper."

Paul did not bring up this matter of money in order to boast about himself. Rather, he was using every means possible to silence the boasting of the Judaizers. Paul knew that not a single person could accuse him of covetousness or selfishness (see Acts 20:33-35, Paul's testimony to the Ephesian church). His hands were clean. He wanted to "cut off" any opportunity for his enemies to accuse him.

The word *chargeable* in 2 Corinthians 11:9 is worth considering in a special way. (See also 12:13-14.) In the Greek, it literally means "to grow numb." The word comes from the image of the electric eel numbing its victim with its shock. A numbed part of the body would be a burden to the victim. Paul had not used any devious tricks to catch the believers by surprise, attack them, or rob them. Both in his preaching of the Gospel and his handling of finances, he was open and honest.

In my own travels, I have seen situations in local churches that have broken my heart. I have seen congregations show little or no appreciation to faithful pastors who were laboring sacrificially to see the church grow. Some of these men were underpaid and overworked, yet the churches seemed to have no love for them. However, their successors were treated like kings! Certainly at the Judgment Seat of Christ, the books will be balanced.

I once heard Dr. W. A. Criswell tell about the faithful missionary couple who returned to the United States on the same ship that brought Teddy Roosevelt home from a safari in Africa. Many reporters and photographers were on the dock, waiting to see Roosevelt and interview him and take pictures; but nobody was on hand to welcome home the veteran missionaries who had spent their lives serving Christ in Africa.

That evening, in their modest hotel room, the couple reviewed their arrival in New York City; and the husband was somewhat bitter.

"It isn't fair," he said to his wife. "Mr. Roosevelt comes home from a hunting trip, and the whole country is out to meet him. We get home after years of service, and nobody was there to greet us."

But his wife had the right answer: "Honey, *we aren't home yet.*"

Paul has presented two pieces of evidence to prove his love for the Corinthians: his jealousy over the church—protecting them from "spiritual unfaithfulness," and his generosity to the church—refusing to accept support from them. He shared a third piece of evidence.

His Anxiety for the Church (2 Cor. 11:16-33)

The key to this long section is verse 28, which could be paraphrased: "Yes, I have been through many trials, but the greatest trial of all, the heaviest burden of all, is my concern for the churches!" The word translated *care* means "pressure, stress, anxiety." The other experiences were external ("without") and occasional, but the burden of the churches was internal and constant.

"We never know the love of our parents for us till we have become parents," said Henry Ward Beecher, and he was right. When our older son was a tot, he pushed a toy into the electric socket and was "zapped" across the room. (We didn't have the word *zap* in those days, but that's still what happened.) One day recently he discovered his own little son playing with the socket, and father's explosive response nearly frightened the child out of a year's growth. "Now I know how you and Mom felt when I was a kid," he told me over the phone. "Being a parent has its fears as well as its joys."

Before listing the various kinds of trials he had experienced, Paul was careful to explain why he was "boasting" in this way. Paul never had any problem boasting about Christ and telling of His sufferings, but he was always hesitant to speak of his own painful experiences as a servant of God. Paul and John the Baptist would have agreed: "He [Christ] must increase, but I must decrease" (John 3:30). "But he that glorieth, let him glory in the Lord" (2 Cor. 10:17).

It was the immature and unspiritual attitude of the Corinthians that forced Paul to write about himself and "glory" (boast) in these experiences. He had begun this section (11:1) by apologizing for his boasting, and he repeated this sentiment in verse 16. In verse 17, Paul was not denying the inspiration of his words; rather, he was admitting that, by boasting, he was being very unlike the Lord. (See 10:1.)

However, he had to do it to prove his love for the Corinthians and protect them from those who would lead them astray.

To begin with, the false teachers were not ashamed to boast, and the Corinthians were not afraid to accept their boasting. "Since boasting is the 'in thing' in your fellowship," Paul seemed to be saying, "then I will boast." Paul may have had the principle of Proverbs 26:5 in mind: "Answer a fool according to his folly, lest he be wise in his own conceit."

Furthermore, Paul was boasting so that he might *help* the church; while the false teachers boasted so that they might "help themselves" to what they could get out of the church. Paul's motive was pure; theirs was selfish. Verse 20 lists the various ways the Judaizers had taken advantage of the church:

Bondage:	They taught a doctrine of legalism that was contrary to the Gospel of grace.
Devour:	They "ate up" all they could get in the church; they took advantage of their privilege of receiving financial support.
Take of you:	"Take you in," fool you. The image is that of a bird caught in a snare or a fish caught on a hook. "They baited you and caught you!"
Exalt:	They exalted themselves, not the Lord Jesus Christ; they loved to be honored and treated as great leaders.
Smite you:	This probably refers to verbal attacks rather than physical violence; the Judaizers did not hesitate to "slap them in the face" and embarrass them in public.

Paul ended this exposure of the unspiritual attitudes and actions of the Judaizers by bringing in some more "inspired irony": "To my shame I admit that we were too weak for that!" (11:21, NIV) The Corinthians thought that Paul's meekness was weakness, when it was really strength. And they thought that the Judaizers' arrogance was power. How ignorant the saints can sometimes be.

When it came to their Jewish heritage, the false teachers were equal to Paul; but when it came to ministry for Christ, it was Paul who was the "super-apostle" and not the Judaizers. Consider what Paul endured for the cause of Christ and the care of the churches.

Sufferings for Christ (2 Cor. 11:23-25a). Had Paul not been an apostle, he would not have experienced these trials. He received "stripes above measure" from both the Gentiles and from the Jews. Three times the Gentiles beat him with rods, and five times he was given 39 lashes by the Jews. Only one beating is recorded in the Book of Acts (16:22), as well as the one stoning (14:19).

Paul knew from the outset of his ministry that he would suffer for Jesus' sake (Acts 9:15-16), and God reaffirmed this to him as his ministry continued (Acts 20:23). He who caused others to suffer for their faith, himself had to suffer for his faith.

Natural hardships (vv. 25b-27). Almost any traveler in that day could have experienced some of these hardships; yet we cannot help but believe that they were caused by the enemy in an attempt to hinder the work of the Lord. Acts 27 records one of the three shipwrecks; we know nothing about the other two. We wonder how many of his precious personal possessions Paul lost in this way.

Because he was constantly on the move, Paul was exposed to the perils of travel. The Judaizers visited the safe places; Paul journeyed to the difficult places. But Paul was no ordinary traveler: he was a marked man. He had enemies among both the Jews and the Gentiles, and some would like to have killed him.

Second Corinthians 11:27 describes the personal consequences of all this difficult travel. In my own limited itinerant ministry, I have had the convenience of automobiles and planes, and yet I must confess that travel wears me out. How much more difficult it was for Paul! No wonder he was filled with weariness and pain. He often had to go without food, drink, and sleep; and sometimes he lacked sufficient clothing to keep himself warm.

While any other traveler could have suffered these things, Paul endured them because of his love for Christ and the church. His greatest burden was not *around* him, but *within* him: the care of all the churches. Why did he care so much? Because he identified with the believers (v. 29). Whatever happened to "his children" touched his own heart and he could not abandon them.

Paul climaxed this narration of his sufferings by telling of his humiliating experience at Damascus, when he—the great apostle—was smuggled out of the city in a basket let over the wall! (vv. 32-33) Would any of the Judaizers ever tell a story like that? Of course not! Even when Paul did narrate his sufferings, he was careful that Christ was glorified, and not Paul.

We cannot read these verses without admiring the courage and devotion of the Apostle Paul. Each trial left its mark on his life, and yet he kept moving on, serving the Lord. "But none of these things move me, neither count I my life dear unto myself" (Acts 20:24).

Paul certainly proved his love for the church.

Now the church had to prove its love for Paul.

May we never take for granted the sacrifices that others have made so that we might enjoy the blessings of the Gospel today.

11

A Preacher in Paradise

2 Corinthians 12:1-10

This section is the climax of Paul's defense of his apostleship and his love for the believers at Corinth. He was reticent to write about these personal experiences, but there was no other way to solve the problem. In fact, to avoid exalting himself, Paul described his experience in the third person rather than the first person. He shared with his readers three experiences from God.

Glory: God Honored Him (2 Cor. 12:1-6)

The Judaizers were anxious to receive honors, and they boasted about their "letters of recommendation (3:1ff). But Paul did not look for honor from men; he let God honor him, for that alone is the honor that really counts.

First, God honored Paul by giving him visions and revelations. Paul saw the glorified Christ on the very day he was converted (Acts 9:3; 22:6). He saw a vision of Ananias coming to minister to him (9:12), and he also had a vision from God when he was called to minister to the Gentiles (22:17).

During his ministry, he had visions from God to guide him and encourage him. It was by a vision that he was called to Macedonia (16:9). When the ministry was difficult in Corinth, God encouraged Paul by a vision (18:9-10). After his arrest in Jerusalem, Paul was again encouraged by a vision from God (23:11). An angel appeared to him in the midst of the storm and assured him that he and the passengers would be saved (27:23).

Along with these special visions that related to his call and ministry, spiritual revelations of divine truth were also communicated to Paul (see Eph. 3:1-6). God gave him a profound understanding of the plan of God for this present age. Certainly Paul understood the mysteries of God.

God also honored Paul by taking him to heaven, and then sending him back to the earth again. This marvelous experience had taken place 14 years before the writing of this letter, which would place it in about the year A.D. 43. This would be the period in Paul's life between his departure for Tarsus (Acts 9:30) and his visit from Barnabas (11:25-26). There is no record of the details of this event, and it is useless for us to speculate.

Jewish rabbis were accustomed to speaking about themselves in the third person, and Paul adopted that approach as he unfolded this experience to his friends (and enemies) at Corinth. So wonderful was this experience that Paul was not quite sure whether God had taken him bodily to heaven, or whether his spirit had left his body. (There is quite a contrast between being "let down" in a basket and being "caught up" to the third heaven!) Paul affirmed here the reality of heaven and the ability of God to take people there. The *third heaven* is the same as "paradise," the heaven of heavens where God dwells in glory. Thanks to modern science, men today have visited the heaven of the clouds (we fly above the clouds) and the heaven of the planets (men have walked on the moon), but man cannot get to God's heaven without God's help.

The interesting thing is that Paul kept quiet about this experience for 14 years! During those years, he was buffeted by his "thorn in the flesh," and perhaps people wondered why he had such a burdensome affliction. The Judaizers may have adopted the views of Job's comforters and said, "This affliction is a punishment from God." (Actually, it was a *gift* from God.) Some of Paul's good friends may have tried to encourage him by saying, "Cheer up, Paul. One day you'll be in heaven!" Paul could have replied, "That's why I have this thorn—I went to heaven!"

God honored Paul by granting him visions and revelations, and by taking him to heaven; but He honored him further by permitting him to hear "unspeakable words" while he was in heaven. He overheard the divine secrets that are shared only in heaven. These things could be spoken by God and by beings in heaven, but they could not be spoken by men.

Could the Judaizers relate any experiences that were like this one? Even Moses, who was intimate with God, met the Lord on the mountaintop; but Paul met the Lord in paradise. Paul had exercised great spiritual discipline during those 14 years, for he had told this experience to no one. There is no doubt that this vision of God's glory was one of the sustaining powers in Paul's life and ministry. No matter where he was— in prison, in the deep, in dangerous travels—he knew that God was with him and that all was well.

You and I are not going to heaven until we die or until our Lord returns. But we have a marvelous encouragement in the fact that we are *today* seated with Christ in the heavenly places (Eph. 2:6). We have a position of authority and victory "far above all" (Eph. 2:21-22). While we have not seen God's glory as Paul did, we do share God's glory now (John 17:22) and one day we shall enter into heaven and behold the glory of Christ (v. 24).

Such an honor as this would have made most people very proud. Instead of keeping quiet for 14 years, they would have immediately told the world and become famous. But Paul did not become proud. He simply told the truth—it was not empty boasting—and let the facts speak for themselves. His great concern was that nobody rob God of the glory and give it to Paul. He wanted others to have an honest estimate of himself and his work (see Rom. 12:3).

How could Paul have such a great experience and still remain humble? Because of the second experience that God brought to his life.

Goodness: God Humbled Him (2 Cor. 12:7-8)

The Lord knows how to balance our lives. If we have only blessings, we may become proud; so He permits us to have burdens as well. Paul's great experience in heaven could have ruined his ministry on earth; so God, in His goodness, permitted Satan to buffet Paul in order to keep him from becoming proud.

The mystery of human suffering will not be solved completely in this life. Sometimes we suffer simply because we are human. Our bodies change as we grow older, and we are susceptible to the normal problems of life. The same body that can bring us pleasures can also bring us pains. The same family members and friends that delight us can also break our hearts. This is a part of the "human comedy," and the only way to escape it is to be less than human. But nobody wants to take that route.

Sometimes we suffer because we are foolish and disobedient to the Lord. Our own rebellion may afflict us, or the Lord may see fit to chasten us in His love (Heb. 12:3ff). King David suffered greatly because of his sin; the consequences were painful and so was the discipline of God (see 2 Sam. 12:1-22; Ps. 51). In His grace, God forgives our sins; but in His government, He must permit us to reap what we sow.

Suffering also is a tool God uses for building godly character (Rom. 5:1-5). Certainly Paul was a man of rich Christian character because he permitted God to mold and make him in the painful experiences of his life. When you walk along the shore of the ocean, you notice that the rocks are sharp in the quiet coves, but polished in those places where the waves beat against them. God can use the "waves and billows" of life to polish us, if we will let Him.

Paul's thorn in the flesh was given to him to keep him from sinning. Exciting spiritual experiences—like going to heaven and back—have a way of inflating the human ego; and pride leads to a multitude of temptations to sin. Had Paul's heart been filled with pride, those next 14 years would have been filled with failure instead of success.

We do not know what Paul's thorn in the flesh was. The word translated *thorn* means "a sharp stake used for torturing or impaling someone." It was a physical affliction of some kind that brought pain and distress to Paul. Some Bible students think that Paul had an eye affliction (see Gal. 6:11); but we cannot know for sure. It is a good thing that we do not know, because no matter what our sufferings may be, we are able to apply the lessons Paul learned and get encouragement.

God permitted Satan to afflict Paul, just as He permitted Satan to afflict Job (see Job 1—2). While we do not fully understand the origin of evil in this universe, or all the purposes God had in mind when He permitted evil to come, we do know that God controls evil and can use it even for His own glory. Satan cannot work against a believer without the permission of God. Everything that the enemy did to Job and

Paul was permitted by the will of God.

Satan was permitted to *buffet* Paul. The word means "to beat, to strike with the fist." The tense of the verb indicates that this pain was either constant or recurring. When you stop to think that Paul had letters to write, trips to take, sermons to preach, churches to visit, and dangers to face as he ministered, you can understand that this was a serious matter. No wonder he prayed three times (as his Lord had done in the Garden [Mark 14:32-41]) that the affliction might be removed from him (2 Cor. 12:8).

When God permits suffering to come to our lives, there are several ways we can deal with it. Some people become bitter and blame God for robbing them of freedom and pleasure. Others just "give up" and fail to get any blessing out of the experience because they will not put any courage into the experience. Still others grit their teeth and put on a brave front, determined to "endure to the very end." While this is a courageous response, it usually drains them of the strength needed for daily living; and after a time, they may collapse.

Was Paul sinning when he prayed to be delivered from Satan's buffeting? I don't think so. It is certainly a normal thing for a Christian to ask God for deliverance from sickness and pain. God has not *obligated* Himself to heal every believer whenever he prays; but He has encouraged us to bring our burdens and needs to Him. Paul did not know whether this "thorn in the flesh" was a temporary testing from God, or a permanent experience he would have to learn to live with.

There are those who want us to believe that an afflicted Christian is a disgrace to God. "If you are obeying the Lord and claiming all that you have in Christ," they say, "then you will never be sick." I have never found that teaching in the Bible. It is true that God promised the Jews special blessing and protection under the Old Covenant (Deut. 7:12ff) but

He never promised the New Testament believers freedom from sickness or suffering. If Paul had access to "instant healing" because of his relationship to Christ, then why didn't he make use of it for himself and for others, such as Epaphroditus? (Phil. 2:25ff)

What a contrast between Paul's two experiences! Paul went from paradise to pain, from glory to suffering. He tasted the blessing of God in heaven and then felt the buffeting of Satan on earth. He went from ecstasy to agony, and yet the two experiences belong together. His one experience of glory prepared him for the constant experience of suffering, for he knew that God was able to meet his need. Paul had gone to heaven—but then he learned that heaven could come to him.

Grace: God Helped Him (2 Cor. 12:9-10)

Two messages were involved in this painful experience. The thorn in the flesh was Satan's message to Paul, but God had another message for him, a message of grace. The tense of the verb in verse 9 is important: "And He [God] has once-for-all said to me." God gave Paul a message that stayed with him. The words Paul heard while in heaven, he was not permitted to share with us; but he did share the words God gave him on earth—and what an encouragement they are.

It was a message of *grace*. What is grace? It is God's provision for our every need when we need it. It has well been said that God in His grace gives us what we do not deserve, and in His mercy He does not give us what we do deserve. Someone has made an acrostic of the word *grace*: **G**od's **R**iches **A**vailable at **C**hrist's **E**xpense. "And of His [Christ's] fullness have all we received, and grace for grace" (John 1:16).

It was a message of *sufficient grace*. There is never a shortage of grace. God is sufficient for our spiritual ministries (2 Cor. 3:4-6) and our material needs (9:8) as well as our physical needs (12:9). If God's grace is sufficient to save us, surely it is sufficient to keep us and strengthen us in our times of suffering.

It was a message of *strengthening grace.* God permits us to become weak so that we might receive His strength. This is a continuous process: "My power is [being] made perfect in [your] weakness" (v. 9, NIV). Strength that knows itself to be strength is actually weakness, but weakness that knows itself to be weakness is actually strength.

In the Christian life, we get many of our blessings through *transformation,* not *substitution.* When Paul prayed three times for the removal of his pain, he was asking God for a substitution: "Give me health instead of sickness, deliverance instead of pain and weakness." Sometimes God does meet the need by substitution; but other times He meets the need by transformation. He does not remove the affliction, but He gives us His grace so that the affliction works *for* us and not *against* us.

As Paul prayed about his problem, God gave him a deeper insight into what He was doing. Paul learned that his thorn in the flesh was *a gift from God.* What a strange gift! There was only one thing for Paul to do: accept the gift from God and allow God to accomplish His purposes. God wanted to keep Paul from being "exalted above measure," and this was His way of accomplishing it.

When Paul accepted his affliction as the gift of God, this made it possible for God's grace to go to work in his life. It was then that God spoke to Paul and gave him the assurance of His grace. Whenever you are going through suffering, spend extra time in the Word of God; and you can be sure God will speak to you. He always has a special message for His children when they are afflicted.

God did not give Paul any explanations; instead, He gave

him a promise: "My grace is sufficient for thee." *We do not live on explanations; we live on promises.* Our feelings change, but God's promises never change. Promises generate faith, and faith strengthens hope.

Paul claimed God's promise and drew upon the grace that was offered to him; this turned seeming tragedy into triumph. God did not change the situation by removing the affliction; He changed it by adding a new ingredient: grace. Our God is "the God of all grace" (1 Peter 5:10), and His throne is a "throne of grace" (Heb. 4:16). The Word of God is "the word of His grace" (Acts 20:32), and the promise is that "He giveth more grace" (James 4:6). No matter how we look at it, God is adequate for every need that we have.

But God does not give us His grace simply that we might "endure" our sufferings. Even unconverted people can manifest great endurance. God's grace should enable us to *rise above* our circumstances and feelings and cause our afflictions to work *for us* in accomplishing positive good. God wants to build our character so that we are more like our Saviour. God's grace enabled Paul not only to accept his afflictions, but to glory in them. His suffering was not a tyrant that controlled him, but a servant that worked for him.

What benefits did Paul receive because of his suffering? For one thing, he experienced the power of Christ in his life. God transformed Paul's weakness into strength. The word translated *rest* means "to spread a tent over." Paul saw his body as a frail tent (2 Cor. 5:1ff), but the glory of God had come into that tent and transformed it into a holy tabernacle.

Something else happened to Paul: he was able to glory in his infirmities. This does not mean that he preferred pain to health, but rather that he knew how to turn his infirmities into assets. What made the difference? The grace of God *and* the glory of God. He "took pleasure" in these trials and problems, not because he was psychologically unbalanced and enjoyed pain, but because he was suffering for the sake of Jesus Christ. He was glorifying God by the way he accepted and handled the difficult experiences of life.

"It is a greater thing to pray for pain's conversion than its removal," wrote P.T. Forsyth, and this is true. Paul won the victory, not by substitution, but by transformation. He discovered the sufficiency of the grace of God.

From Paul's experience, we may learn several practical lessons.

1. *The spiritual is far more important to the dedicated believer than the physical.* This is not to suggest that we ignore the physical, because our bodies are the temples of the Spirit of God. But it does mean that we try not to make our bodies an end in themselves. They are God's tools for accomplishing His work in this world. What God does in developing our Christian character is far more valuable than physical healing without character.

2. *God knows how to balance burdens and blessings, suffering and glory.* Life is something like a prescription: the individual ingredients might hurt us, but when properly blended, they help us.

3. *Not all sickness is caused by sin.* The argument of Job's comforters was that Job had sinned, and that was why he was suffering. But their argument was wrong in Job's case, as well as in Paul's case. There are times when God permits Satan to afflict us so that God might accomplish a great purpose in our lives.

4. *There is something worse than sickness, and that is sin; and the worst sin of all is pride.* The healthy person who is rebelling against God is in worse shape than the suffering person who is submitting to God and enjoying God's grace. It is a paradox—and an evidence of the sovereignty of God—that

God used Satan, the proudest of all beings, to help keep Paul humble.

5. *Physical affliction need not be a barrier to effective Christian service.* Today's saints are too prone to pamper themselves and use every little ache or pain as an excuse to stay home from church or refuse to accept opportunities for service. Paul did not permit his thorn in the flesh to become a stumbling block. In fact, he let God turn that thorn into a stepping-stone.

6. *We can always rest in God's Word.* He always has a message of encouragement for us in times of trial and suffering.

The great French mystic, Madame Guyon, once wrote to a suffering friend, "Ah, if you knew what power there is in an accepted sorrow!"

Paul knew about that power, because he trusted the will of God and depended on the grace of God.

That same power can be yours today.

12

Three to Get Ready!

2 Corinthians 12:11—13:14

As Paul brought his letter to a close, his great love for the Corinthians constrained him to make one last appeal. He did not want his third visit to their church to be another painful experience for them and for him. He had opened his heart to them, explained his ministry, answered their accusations, and urged them to submit to the Word of God and obey the Lord. What more could he say or do?

In this closing section of the letter, Paul used three approaches in his attempt to motivate the Corinthians toward obedience and submission.

He Shamed Them (2 Cor. 12:11-21)
When we were children, how many times did we hear, "Shame on you!" from a parent or a neighbor? It is a good thing when people can be ashamed of their bad actions or attitudes. It is evidence of a hard heart and a calloused conscience when a guilty person no longer feels shame. "Were they ashamed when they had committed abomination? Nay,

143

they were not at all ashamed, neither could they blush" (Jer. 6:15).

First, Paul shamed the Corinthians for their *lack of commendation* (2 Cor. 12:11-13). They should have been boasting about him instead of compelling him to boast. Instead, the Corinthians were boasting about the "super-apostles," the Judaizers who had won their affection and were now running their church.

Was Paul inferior to these men? In no way! The Corinthians had seen Paul in action; in fact, they owed their very souls to him. He had done among them the miraculous signs that proved his apostleship (Heb. 2:1-4). He had persevered in his ministry at Corinth in spite of external persecution and internal problems. He had cost the church nothing. Paul used his subtle irony again when he wrote, "How were you inferior to the other churches, except that I was never a burden to you? Forgive me this wrong!" (2 Cor. 12:13, NIV)

One of the dangers of the Christian life is that of getting accustomed to our blessings. A godly pastor or Sunday School teacher can do so much for us that we begin to take the ministry for granted. (To be fair, I must admit that pastors are sometimes guilty of taking their church members for granted.) This attitude led Paul to shame them for their *lack of appreciation* (vv. 14-18).

In spite of the difficulties involved, Paul had been faithful to visit the Corinthians; and now he was about to make his third visit (see 13:1). Instead of being grateful, the Corinthians criticized Paul for changing his plans. Paul had taken no support from the church, but rather had given sacrificially for the church; yet they were unwilling to show their appreciation by sharing with others. It seemed that the more Paul loved them, the less they loved Paul! Why? Because they did not have a sincere love for Christ (11:3). Paul was willing to "spend and expend" in order to help the church.

The Judaizers had used crafty methods in order to exploit the church (see 4:2), but Paul had been open and without guile. The only "trick" Paul had played on them was his refusal to receive financial support. In this, he disarmed them so that they could never accuse him of being interested only in money. None of the associates that Paul sent to them exploited them in any way or took advantage of them.

It is a tragic thing when children do not appreciate what their parents do for them. It is also a tragedy when God's children fail to appreciate what their "spiritual parents" do for them. What is the cause of this *lack of appreciation?* Paul dealt with it in the next paragraph: *lack of consecration* (vv. 19-21). There were terrible sins in the church, and Paul wanted them judged and put away before he came for his visit. Otherwise, his visit would just be another painful experience.

Some of the church members were probably saying, "If Paul visits us again, he will just create more problems!" Paul made it clear that his desire was to *solve* problems and strengthen the church. Sins in the church must be faced honestly and dealt with courageously. To "sweep them under the rug" is to make matters worse. Sin in the church is like cancer in the human body: it must be cut out.

Consider the sins that the church was guilty of, sins that should have been confessed and put away. They were guilty of quarreling (debates) because they envied one another. They had sudden explosions of anger (wraths). They promoted carnal intrigues and plots in the church (strifes), which involved backbitings and whisperings. All of this was born out of pride and an exaggerated sense of importance (swellings) and resulted in disorder in the church (tumults) (2 Cor. 12:20). If you will compare this list of sins with 1 Corinthians

13, you will see that there was a lack of love in the congregation.

Along with these "sins of the spirit" (7:1), there were also gross sins of the flesh—fornication and lasciviousness (debauchery). Paul had dealt with these sins in 1 Corinthians 5—6, but some of the offenders had persisted in their disobedience. They were permitting their old life to take over again (1 Cor. 6:9-11), instead of yielding to the new life.

Paul did not eagerly anticipate this third visit. He feared that he would not find the church as he wanted it to be, and that they would not find him as they wanted him to be. But Paul promised them that, though he would be humbled and grieved (the word means "to grieve for the dead"), he would still use his authority to straighten things out. His love for them was too great for him to ignore these problems and permit them to continue to weaken the church.

The Corinthians should have been ashamed, but they were not. To assure that he would get his message across, Paul used a second approach.

He Warned Them (2 Cor. 13:1-8)

There are two warnings here.

"Prepare yourselves!" (2 Cor. 13:1-4) In dealing with sin in a local church, we must have facts and not rumors. Paul quoted Deuteronomy 19:15, and we find parallels in Numbers 35:30 and Matthew 18:16, as well as 1 Timothy 5:19. The presence of witnesses would help to guarantee the truth about a matter, especially when the church members were at such variance with one another.

Had the church members followed the instructions given by Jesus in Matthew 18:15-20, they would have solved most of their problems themselves. I have seen small disagreements in a church grow into large and complicated problems, only because the believers did not obey our Lord's directions. The pastor and congregation must not get involved in a matter until the individuals involved have sincerely sought a solution.

The Judaizers in the church had accused Paul of being a weak man (see 2 Cor. 10:7-11). Their approach to ministry was heavy-handed and dictatorial, while Paul's was gentle and humble (see 1:24). Now Paul assured them that he would show them how strong he could be—*if* that is what it took to solve the problems. "I will not spare!" was his warning, and he used a word that means "to spare in battle." In short, Paul was declaring war on anybody who opposed the authority of God's Word.

"Let Paul prove he is a true apostle!" said his opponents. Paul's reply was, "Like Jesus Christ, I am strong when it appears I am weak." On the cross, Jesus Christ manifested weakness; but the cross is still "the power of God" (1 Cor. 1:18). Paul had already explained his method of spiritual warfare (2 Cor. 10:1-6) and had cautioned his readers not to look on the surface of things, but to look deeper.

By the standards of the world, both Jesus and Paul were weak; but by the standards of the Lord, both were strong. It is a wise and mature worker who knows when to be "weak" and when to be "strong" as he deals with the discipline problems in the local church.

A pastor friend of mine, now in heaven, had a quiet manner of delivery in the pulpit, and a similar approach in his personal ministry. After hearing him preach, a visitor said, "I kept waiting for him to start preaching!" She was accustomed to hearing a loud preacher who generated more heat than light. But my friend built a strong church because he knew the true standards for ministry. He knew how to be "weak in Christ" and also how to be "strong."

How do people measure the ministry today? By powerful

oratory or biblical content? By Christian character or what the press releases say? Too many Christians follow the world's standards when they evaluate ministries, and they need to pay attention to God's standards.

"Examine yourselves!" (2 Cor. 13:5-8) This paragraph is an application of the word *proof* that Paul used in verse 3. "You have been examining me," wrote Paul, "but why don't you take time to examine yourselves?" I have noticed in my ministry that those who are quick to examine and condemn others are often guilty of worse sins themselves. In fact, one way to make yourself look better is to condemn somebody else.

To begin with, Paul told the Corinthians that they should examine their hearts to see if they were really born again and members of the family of God. Do you have the witness of the Holy Spirit in your heart? (Rom. 8:9,16) Do you love the brethren? (1 John 3:14) Do you practice righteousness? (1 John 2:29; 3:9) Have you overcome the world so that you are living a life of godly separation? (1 John 5:4) These are just a few of the tests we can apply to our own lives to be certain that we are the children of God.

In one of the churches I pastored, we had a teenager who was the center of every problem in the youth group. He was a gifted musician and a member of the church, but nevertheless he was a problem. One summer when he went off to our church youth camp, the youth leaders and church officers and I agreed together to pray for him daily. At one of the meetings, he got up and announced that he had been saved that week! His Christian profession up to that time had been counterfeit. He experienced a dramatic change in his life, and today he is serving the Lord faithfully.

No doubt many of the problems in the church at Corinth were caused by people who professed to be saved, but who had never repented and trusted Jesus Christ. Our churches are filled with such people today. Paul called such people *reprobate*, which means "counterfeit, discredited after a test." Paul used this word again in 2 Corinthians 13:6-7, emphasizing the fact that it is important for a person to know for sure that he is saved and going to heaven (see 1 John 5:11-13).

In verse 7, Paul made it clear that he did not want the Corinthians to fail the test just to prove that he was right. Nor did he want them to live godly lives just so he could boast about them. He did not mind being despised and criticized for their sakes, so long as they were obeying the Lord. He was not concerned about his own reputation, for the Lord knew his heart; but he was concerned about their Christian character.

The important thing is the truth of the Gospel and the Word of God (v. 8). Paul did not state here that it is impossible to attack the truth or hinder the truth, for these things were going on at that time in the Corinthian church. He was affirming that he and his associates wanted the truth to prevail, come what may, and that they were determined to further the truth, not obstruct it. In the end, God's truth will prevail, so why try to oppose it? "There is no wisdom nor understanding nor counsel against the Lord" (Prov. 21:30).

He Encouraged Them (2 Cor. 13:9-14)

To begin with, Paul encouraged the Corinthians by his personal prayers on their behalf (v. 9). The word translated *wish* in the *King James Version* carries the meaning of "pray." Paul prayed for their *perfection*, which does not mean absolute sinless perfection, but "spiritual maturity." The word is part of a word family in the Greek that means "to be fitted out, to be equipped." As a medical term, it means "to set a broken bone, to adjust a twisted limb." It also means "to outfit a ship for a voyage" and "to equip an army for battle." In Matthew 4:21, it is translated "mending nets."

One of the ministries of our risen Lord is that of perfecting His people (Heb. 13:20-21). He uses the Word of God (2 Tim. 3:16-17) in the fellowship of the local church (Eph. 4:11-16) to equip His people for life and service. He also uses suffering as a tool to equip us (1 Peter 5:10). As Christians pray for one another (1 Thes. 3:10) and personally assist one another (Gal. 6:1, where "restore" is this same word *perfect*), the exalted Lord ministers to His church and makes them fit for ministry.

Balanced Christian growth and ministry is impossible in isolation. Someone has said that you can no more raise one Christian than you can raise one bee. Christians belong to each other and need each other. A baby must grow up in a loving family if it is to be balanced and normal. The emphasis today on the "individual Christian" as apart from his place in a local assembly, is wrong and very dangerous. We are sheep, and we must flock together. We are members of the same body, and we must minister to one another.

In 2 Corinthians 13:10, Paul gave the Corinthians a second encouragement—the Word of God. Paul wrote this letter to meet the immediate needs of a local congregation, but we today benefit from it because it is a part of the inspired Word of God. This letter carries the same authority as the presence of the apostle himself. Paul's great desire was that the congregation's obedience to the letter solve their problems, so that he would not have to exercise authority when he visited them.

Sometimes the minister of the Word must tear down before he can build up. (See Jer. 1:7-10.) The farmer must pull up the weeds before he can plant the seeds and get a good crop. Paul had to tear down the wrong thinking in the minds of the Corinthians (2 Cor. 10:4-6) before he could build up the truth in their hearts and minds. The negative attitude of the

Corinthians made it necessary for Paul to *destroy*, but his great desire was to *build*.

In my own ministry, I have been through two building programs and two remodeling programs and, in spite of all their demands, building programs to me are much easier. It is much simpler and less expensive to build a new structure on unimproved land than to tear down walls and try to remodel an old building. Likewise, it is much easier to take a new believer and teach him the Word than it is to try to change the wrong thinking of an older saint. Wrong ideas can "hold out" against the truth for a long time, until the Spirit of God demolishes the walls in the mind.

Paul encouraged the saints *to cultivate grace, love, and peace* (vv. 11-12). The word translated *farewell* means "grace," a common form of greeting in that day. It can also be translated *rejoice.* The command *be perfect* relates to Paul's prayer in verse 9 and carries the idea "be mature, be restored and fitted for life." *Be of good comfort* means "be encouraged." In spite of all their sins and problems, they had every right to be encouraged.

Live in peace was a needed admonition, for there were divisions and dissensions in the church (see 12:20). If they practiced love and sought to be of one mind, the wars would cease and they would enjoy peace in their fellowship. To *be of one mind* does not mean that we all agree on everything, but that we agree not to disagree over matters that are not essential.

Our God is the "God of love and peace" (13:11). Can the outside world tell that from the way we live and the way we conduct the business of the church? "Behold how they love one another!" was what the lost world said about the early church, but it has been a long time since the church has earned that kind of commendation.

Since ancient times, the kiss has been a form of greeting and a gesture of love and fellowship. However, it was usually exchanged between members of the same sex. The early church used the *kiss of peace* and *kiss of love* as evidences of their affection and concern for one another. It was a "holy kiss," sanctified because of their devotion to Jesus Christ. It was not unusual for members of the early church to kiss new believers after their baptism and thus to welcome them into the fellowship.

The everyday fellowship of God's people is important to the church. We must greet each other in other places as well as the fellowship of the assembly, and we must show concern for each other. In giving this admonition in verse 12, Paul was certainly hitting hard at one of the most serious problems in the church: their division and lack of concern for one another.

The closing benediction in verse 14 is one of the most beloved used in the church. It emphasizes the Trinity (see Matt. 28:19) and the blessings we can receive because we belong to God. *The grace of our Lord Jesus Christ* reminds us of His birth, when He became poor in order to make us rich (see 2 Cor. 8:9). The *love of God* takes us to Calvary where God gave His Son as the sacrifice for our sins (John 3:16). The *communion of the Holy Ghost* reminds us of Pentecost, when the Spirit of God came and formed the church (Acts 2).

The Corinthian believers then, and all believers now, desperately needed the blessings of grace, love, and communion. The Judaizers then, and the cultists today, emphasize law instead of grace, exclusiveness instead of love, and independence rather than communion (fellowship). The competition in the Corinthian church, resulting in divisions, would have been solved if the people had only lived by God's grace and love.

The church is a miracle, and it can be sustained only by the miracle ministry of God. No amount of human skill, talents, or programs can make the church what it ought to be. Only God can do that. If each believer is depending on the grace of God, walking in the love of God, and participating in the fellowship of the Spirit, not walking in the flesh, then he will be a part of the answer and not a part of the problem. He will be *living* this benediction—and being a benediction to others!

Ask God to make you that kind of Christian.

Be encouraged—and then encourage others.